SERENDIPITIES

Italian Academy Lectures

The
Italian
Academy

SERENDIPITIES

LANGUAGE & LUNACY

Umberto Eco

TRANSLATED BY WILLIAM WEAVER

COLUMBIA UNIVERSITY PRESS   NEW YORK

Columbia University Press
Publishers Since 1893
New York   Chichester, West Sussex

Translation copyright © 1998 Umberto Eco
All rights reserved
Library of Congress Cataloging-in-Publication Data
Eco, Umberto.
[Essays. English. Selections]
Serendipities : language and lunacy / Umberto Eco ; translated by
William Weaver.
p. cm. — (Italian Academy lectures)
Includes index.
ISBN 0-231-11134-7
1. Language and languages—Philosophy. 2. Intercultural
communication. I. Weaver, William, 1923– . II. Title.
III. Series.
P106.E29 1998
401—dc21   98–7935

Designed by Linda Secondari

Printed in the United States of America

c 10 9 8 7 6 5 4 3 2

CONTENTS |

Preface   *vii*

1 | THE FORCE OF FALSITY   1

2 | LANGUAGES IN PARADISE   23

3 | FROM MARCO POLO TO LEIBNIZ   53
   Stories of Intellectual Misunderstandings

4 | THE LANGUAGE OF THE AUSTRAL LAND   77

5 | THE LINGUISTICS OF JOSEPH DE MAISTRE   97

Notes   *117*

Index   *121*

PREFACE |

In the introduction to my *Search for a Perfect Language* (1995), I
informed the reader that, bearing in mind the physical limits of a
book, I had been forced to omit many curious episodes, and I concluded:"I console myself that I have the material for future excursions in erudition" (6).

I made some of these excursions subsequently, and two of them
were the subject of two lectures I gave during my term as Fellow
in Residence at the Italian Academy for Advanced Studies at
Columbia University in New York (October–December 1996); of
these, I have included in this collection only one, the third essay.
The second piece in this volume, on the languages of Paradise, I
read in April 1997 at a colloquium held in Jerusalem on the concept of Paradise in the three monotheistic religions. The papers on
Gabriel de Foigny and Joseph de Maistre were published in Italian
in two collections dedicated to the memory of Luigi Rosiello. All
these essays have been revised for the present volume, even though
I could not avoid some repetition (which will be convenient, however, for the reader who does not read the chapters from the first
to the last).

In collecting these pieces I saw that not only are they parts of
the history of the search for a perfect language but they also have
something else in common: they speak of *errors* (such as the
European incomprehension of non-European languages or the
mystical-reactionary view of language in Maistre, which leads him
to absolutely risible etymological games) or else of *fictional inven-*

tions (as in the case of the Austral language of Foigny, who tells a story that today we would call science fiction but in its own day belonged to the utopian genre). Dante's case is a bit different: in reconstructing the situation of Adam in Paradise, the poet perhaps presumed he was telling the truth, but he devised his linguistic model as justification for his poetic activity, and to some extent he adjusted the story to his own purpose, proposing himself as the new Adam. Dante's story, however, is even more complex: on the one hand, we suspect that, more or less consciously, he was borrowing ideas from the cabalistic tradition; on the other, we find it curious how some interpreters have got things wrong and have even committed the unforgivable error of believing Dante had the King James Bible at his elbow. And, finally, this story shows how theories can change according to the translation of the Bible that the theorists have at their disposal.

In short, all these erudite excursions of mine are concerned with a linguistics that I would call "lunatic," and—as I have already said in my book on perfect languages—even the most lunatic experiments can produce strange side effects, stimulating research that proves perhaps less amusing but scientifically more serious.

For this reason, in collecting these essays, I have decided to precede them with a lecture I gave at the University of Bologna for the opening of the 1994–95 academic year. The polemical title is "The Force of Falsity," and in the lecture I wanted to show how a number of ideas that today we consider false actually changed the world (sometimes for the better, sometimes for the worse) and how, in the best instances, false beliefs and discoveries totally without credibility could then lead to the discovery of something true (or at least something we consider true today). In the field of the sciences, this mechanism is known as serendipity. An excellent example of it is given us by Columbus, who—believing he could reach the Indies by sailing westward—actually discovered America, which he had not intended to discover.

But the concept of serendipity can be broadened. A mistaken project does not always lead to something correct: often (and this is what happened in many projected perfect languages) a project that the author believed right seems to us unrealizable, but for this very reason we understand why something else was right. Take the case of Foigny: he invents a language that cannot work, and he invents it deliberately to parody other languages seriously proposed. But in doing so he helps us see (probably beyond his own intentions) why, on the contrary, the imperfect languages we all speak work fairly well.

In other words, I feel that what links the essays collected here is that they are about ideas, projects, beliefs that exist in a twilight zone between common sense and lunacy, truth and error, visionary intelligence and what now seems to us stupidity, though it was not stupid in its day and we must therefore reconsider it with great respect.

SERENDIPITIES

1 | THE FORCE OF FALSITY

In the *Quaestio quodlibetalis* XII, 14, Saint Thomas declares "utrum veritas sit fortior inter vinum et regem et mulierem," raising, that is, the question of which is more powerful, more convincing, more constrictive: the power of the king, the influence of wine, the charms of woman, or the strength of truth.

Aquinas's reply respected the king, at whose table he did not, I believe, reject a few good glasses of wine, though he proved he could resist woman's charms by pursuing with a glowing firebrand the naked courtesan his brothers had introduced into his room to convince him to become a Benedictine rather than dishonor the family by taking the mendicant habit of the Dominicans. As usual, his reply was subtle and articulated: wine, monarch, woman, and truth are not comparable because *non sunt unius generis* (they do not belong to the same category). But if we consider them *per comparationem ad aliquem effectum* (insofar as their effects are concerned), all can stir the human heart to some action. Wine acts on our corporal aspect because it produces drunkenness, and over our sensitive animal nature the *delectatio venerea*—woman, in short—has power (Thomas did not conceive of possible sexual impulses in the opposite direction that might legitimately affect woman, but we cannot ask Thomas to be Héloise). As for the practical intellect, it is obvious that the king's will has power over it, the

* A first version was given as a prolusion at the opening of the Academic Year, Bologna, 1994–95.

command of law. But the only force that moves the speculative intellect is truth. And inasmuch as *vires corporales subjiciuntur viribus animalibus, vires animales intellectualibus, et intellectuales practicae speculativis . . . idea simpliciter veritas dignior est et excellentior et fortior* (as our corporeal forces depend on the animal ones, and the animal on the intellectual—and so on and so forth—thus truth is stronger than anything else).

Such then is the force of truth. But experience teaches us that often the imposition of truth has been delayed, and its acceptance has come at the price of blood and tears. Is it not possible that a similar force is displayed also by misunderstanding, whereby we can legitimately speak of a force of the false?

To demonstrate that the false (not necessarily in the form of lies but surely in the form of error) has motivated many events of history, I should rely on a criterion of truth. But if I were to choose it too dogmatically, I would risk ending my argument at the very moment I begin it.

Belief in gods, of whatever description, has motivated human history, thus if it were argued that all myths, all revelations of every religion, are nothing but lies, one could only conclude that for millennia we have lived under the dominion of the false.

But in reaching this conclusion, we would be indulging in more than just banal euhemerism: this same skeptical argument would seem singularly akin to the opposing fideistic argument. If we believe in any revealed religion and, for instance, we have to admit that Christ is the son of God, then he is not the Messiah still awaited in Jerusalem. And if Mohammed is the prophet of Allah, then it is mistaken to offer sacrifices to the Plumed Serpent. If we follow the most enlightened and indulgent of deisms, prepared to believe at once in the Communion of Saints and the Great Wheel of the Tao, then we will reject, as fruit of error, the massacre of infidels and heretics. If we are worshipers of Satan, we will consider puerile the Sermon on the Mount. If we are radical atheists, every faith will be nothing but misunderstanding. Therefore, given that in the course of history many have acted on beliefs in which many others did not believe, we must perforce admit that for each, to a different degree, history has been largely the Theater of an Illusion.

So let us espouse a less contested notion of truth and falsehood, even if it is philosophically debatable (if we listen to philosophers, we must debate everything, and there would be no end to the discussion). Let us adopt the criterion of scientific or historical truth accepted by Western culture: namely, the criterion thanks to which we all agree that Julius Caesar was killed on the Ides of March, that on 19 October 1781 the troops of General Lord Cornwallis surrendered at Yorktown to George Washington, ending the American Revolution, that sulphuric acid is H_2SO_4, and that the dolphin is a mammal.

Naturally each of these notions is subject to revision on the basis of new discoveries, but for the moment they all are recorded in the encyclopedia, and until proved otherwise we believe, as factual truth, that the chemical composition of water is H_2O (and some philosophers hold that such a truth must be valid in all possible worlds).

At this point it can be said that, over the course of history, beliefs and affirmations that today's encyclopedia categorically denies have been given credence and indeed believed so completely as to subjugate the learned, generate and destroy empires, inspire poets (not always witnesses to the truth), and drive human beings to heroic sacrifices, intolerance, massacre, the quest for knowledge. If this is true, how can we not assert that a Force of the False exists?

Ptolemy

The virtually canonical example is the Ptolemaic system. Today we know that for centuries humankind acted on its belief in a false representation of the cosmos. People sought out every possible argument that could compensate for the falsity of the image; they invented epicycles and deferents; finally, with Tycho Brahe, they tried to move all the planets around the sun, while allowing the sun to continue moving around the earth. On the basis of the

Ptolemaic image not only did Dante Alighieri act (small harm done), but, worse, so did the Phoenician navigators, Saint Brendan, Eric the Red, and Christopher Columbus (and one of them was somehow the first to arrive in America). And further, on the basis of this false hypothesis, people managed to divide the globe into parallels and meridian degrees, as we still do, having simply shifted the prime meridian from the Canaries to Greenwich.

The example of Ptolemy, which, by association, immediately calls up the unfortunate story of Galileo, would seem to suggest that, with secular arrogance, I confine my history of the power of falsehood to instances where dogmatic thought rejected the light of truth. But here is a story from the opposite position, the story of another falsity, slowly constructed by modern secular thought to defame religious thought.

The Flat Earth

Try this experiment. Ask an ordinary person what Christopher Columbus wanted to prove when he set out to reach the Orient by way of the Occident and what it was that the learned men of Salamanca stubbornly denied, trying to prevent his voyage. The reply, in most cases, will be that Columbus believed the earth was round, whereas the Salamanca sages believed it was flat and hence thought that, after sailing a short distance, the three caravels would plunge into the cosmic abyss.

Nineteenth-century secular thought, irritated by the Church's refusal to accept the heliocentric hypothesis, attributed to all Christian thought (patristic and scholastic) the idea that the earth was flat. The nineteenth-century positivist and anticlerical made a meal of this cliché, which, as Jeffrey Burton Russell has demonstrated,[1] was strengthened during the battle the supporters of Darwinian theory joined against every form of fundamentalism. It was a matter of demonstrating that, as the churches had erred about the sphericity of the earth, so they could err also about the origin of species.

The Darwinians then exploited the fact that a Christian author of the fourth century, such as Lactantius in his *Institutiones divinae*, having to accept many biblical passages in which the universe is described as modeled on the tabernacle, hence quadrangular in form, opposed the pagan theories of the earth's roundness, also because he could not accept the idea that there existed antipodes where men would have to walk with their heads down and their feet in the air.

Finally it was discovered that a Byzantine geographer of the fourth century, Cosmas Indicopleustes, had argued that the cosmos was rectangular, with an arc that dominated the flat pavement of the earth (once again the archetype was the tabernacle). In his authoritative book *History of Planetary Systems from Thales to Kepler*, J. L. E. Dreyer admits that Cosmas was not an official representative of the Church, while giving ample space to his theory. E. J. Dijksterhuis, in his *Mechanization of the World Picture* (originally in Dutch), asserts that the theory of Cosmas remained the prevalent opinion for many centuries, even though he also concedes that Lactantius and Cosmas must not be considered representatives of the scientific culture of the Church Fathers.[2]

The fact is that Christian culture, in the early years and in the Middle Ages, left Lactantius to stew in his own juice, and the text of Cosmas, written in Greek and therefore in a language the Christian Middle Ages had forgotten, was revealed to the Western world only in 1706, in Montfaucon's *Nova collectio patrum et scriptorum graecorum*. No medieval author knew Cosmas, and his text was considered an authority of the "Dark Ages" only after its English publication in 1897!

Naturally Ptolemy knew the earth was round, otherwise he would not have been able to divide it into three hundred and sixty degrees of meridian. Eratosthenes also knew it, for in the third century before Christ he calculated with reasonable accuracy the diameter of the earth. Pythagoras knew it, too, as did Parmenides, Eudoxius, Plato, Aristotle, Euclid, Aristarchus, and Archimedes. And it turns out that the only ones who did not believe it were two materialists, Leucippus and Democritus.

Macrobius and Martianus Capella were also well aware that the earth was round. As for the Church Fathers, they had to deal with the biblical text, which spoke of that tiresome tabernacle form, but Augustine, even if he did not have firm notions on the subject, knew those of the ancients and conceded that the sacred text was speaking metaphorically. His position is somewhat different, though fairly common in patristic thought: as knowledge of the earth's form will not save the soul, the question seemed to him of scant interest. Isidore of Seville (who was surely not a model of scientific precision) calculates at a certain point that the equator was eighty thousand stadii in length. Could he have thought the earth was flat?

Even a high school student can easily deduce that, if Dante enters the funnel of the Inferno and emerges on the other side to see unknown stars at the foot of the mount of Purgatory, then he must have known very well that the earth was round. But forget Dante, to whom we have a tendency to attribute every virtue. The fact is that Origen and Ambrose were of the same opinion, and in the scholastic age a spherical earth was conceived and spoken of by Albertus Magnus and Thomas Aquinas, Roger Bacon, John of Holywood, Pierre d'Ailly, Egidius Romanus, Nicolas Oresme, and Jean Buridan, to name only a few.

So what was the big argument all about in the time of Columbus? The sages of Salamanca had, in fact, made calculations more precise than his, and they held that the earth, while assuredly round, was far more vast than the Genoese navigator believed, and therefore it was mad for him to attempt to circumnavigate it in order to reach the Orient by way of the Occident. Columbus, on the contrary, burning with a sacred fire, good navigator but bad astronomer, thought the earth smaller than it was. Naturally neither he nor the learned men of Salamanca suspected that between Europe and Asia there lay another continent. And so you see how complicated life is, and how fragile are the boundaries between truth and error, right and wrong. Though they were right, the sages of Salamanca were wrong; and Columbus, while he was wrong, pursued faithfully his error and proved to be right—thanks to serendipity.

But read what Andrew Dickson White says in his *History of the Warfare of Science with Theology in Christendom*.[3] True, in these two thick volumes his aim is to list every instance in which religious thought impeded the advancement of science, but as he is an informed and honest man he cannot conceal the fact that Augustine, Albertus Magnus, and Aquinas knew very well that the earth was round. He adds, however, that to sustain this idea, they had to combat dominant theological thought. But dominant theological thought was represented, in fact, by Augustine, Albertus, and Aquinas, who thus had to combat no one.

It is again Russell who reminds us that a serious text like that of F. S. Marvin appearing in *Studies in the History and in the Method of Sciences* repeats that "Ptolemy's maps . . . were forgotten in the West for a thousand years" and that a manual of 1988 (A. Holt-Jensen's *Geography: Its History and Concepts*) states that the medieval Church taught that the earth was a flat disk with Jerusalem at its center. Even Daniel Boorstin, in his popular book *The Discoverers*, says that from the fourth to the fourteenth century Christianity had suppressed the notion of the earth's being round.[4]

From Constantine to Prester John

Another falsehood that changed world history? The Donation of Constantine. Today, thanks to Lorenzo Valla, we know that the Donation was not authentic. And yet, without that document, without a profound belief in its authenticity, European history would have followed a different course: no conflict over investitures, no mortal struggle for the Holy Roman Empire, no temporal power of the popes, no slap at Agnani, but also no Sistine Chapel, which was created after the Donation was called into question but could still be constructed because for centuries the Donation continued to be thought genuine.

In the second half of the twelfth century a letter arrived in the West, telling how in the far-off East, beyond the regions occupied by the Mussulmen, beyond those lands the crusaders had tried to wrest from the dominion of the infidel only to see them returned to that same rule, there was a flourishing Christian region, governed by a legendary priest John, or Presbyter Johannes, or Prester John, *re potentia et virtute dei et domini nostri Iesu Christi.* The letter began by saying:

know and believe firmly that I, Priest John, am lord of lords; and in every wealth that exists beneath the sky, as also in strength and power I surpass all the kings of the earth. Seventy-two monarchs pay us tribute. I am a devout Christian and everywhere I defend and support with alms the true Christians governed by the dominion of my Clemency. . . .

Our sovereignty extends over the three Indias: from the greater India, where rests the body of the apostle Thomas, our domains extend into the desert and press the confines of the Orient, then turn toward the Occident as far as Babylonia Deserta, by the tower of Babel. . . . In our domains live elephants, dromedaries, camels, hippopotami, crocodiles, *metagallinari, cametennus, tinsirete,* panthers, onagers, red and white lions, white bears and blackbirds, mute cicadas, gryphos, tigers, jackals, hyenas, wild oxen, centaurs, wild men, horned men, fauns, centaurs and women of the same species, pygmies, men with dogs' heads, giants forty cubits tall, monocles, cyclops, a bird called the phoenix, and almost every kind of animal that lives beneath the vault of the heavens. . . . In one of our provinces the river known as Indus flows. . . . This river, whose source is in Paradise, winds its way along various branches through the entire province and in it are found natural stones, emeralds, sapphires, carbuncles, topazes, chrysolytes, onyx, beryl, amethyst, sardonics, and many other precious stones. . . .

In the extreme regions of the land . . . we possess an island
. . . where throughout the year, twice a week, God causes an
abundant rain of manna to fall, which the people gather and
eat, nor do they subsist on any other food save this. In fact, they
do not plow, do not sow, do not reap, nor stir the earth in any
way to extract its richest fruit from it. . . . All of them, who are
fed only on celestial food, live five hundred years. Still, on
reaching the age of one hundred, they are rejuvenated and re-
gain strength, drinking three times the water of a spring that
rises at the root of a tree that is found in that place. . . . Amongst
us no one lies. . . . Amongst us none is an adulterer. No vice
has power in our midst.[5]

In the course of the following centuries—until the seventeenth—translated and paraphrased many times into various languages and versions, the letter had a decisive importance in the expansion of the Christian West toward the Orient. The idea that
beyond the Moslem territories there could be a Christian kingdom
justified all ventures of expansion and exploration. Prester John was
discussed by Pian del Carpine, William of Rubruck, and Marco
Polo. Around the middle of the fourteenth century the kingdom of
Prester John shifted from a vague Orient toward Ethiopia, as the
Portuguese navigators began their African explorations. Attempts
to communicate with John were made in the fifteenth century by
Henry IV of England, by the duc de Berry, by Pope Eugene IV. In
Bologna, at the time of the coronation of Charles V, there was still
talk of Prester John as a possible ally in the reconquest of the Holy
Sepulcher.

Where did Prester John's letter come from? What was its purpose? Perhaps it was a document of anti-Byzantine propaganda,
produced in the scriptoria of Frederick I. But the problem is not
so much its origin (fakes of every description were abundant at
that time) as its reception. The geographical fantasy gradually generated a political project. In other words, the phantom called up
by some scribe with a knack for counterfeiting documents (a

highly respected literary activity of the period) served as an alibi for the expansion of the Christian world toward Africa and Asia, a welcome argument favoring the white man's burden.[6]

From the Rosicrucians to the *Protocols*

Another invention also rich in historic results was the Confraternity of the Rosy Cross. Many writers have depicted the atmosphere of extraordinary spiritual renewal that developed at the beginning of the seventeenth century, when the idea of the beginning of a Golden Age emerged. This climate of expectancy pervades in various forms (in a play of mutual influences) both the Catholic world and the Protestant: plans of ideal republics were elaborated, from Campanella's *City of the Sun* to the *Christianopolis* of Johann Valentin Andrae, aspirations to a universal monarchy, to a general renovation of behavior and of religious sensibility, just when Europe, in the period around the Thirty Years' War, was ablaze with national conflicts, religious hatreds, and the assertion of the raison d'état.

In 1614 a manifesto appeared, entitled *Fama Fraternitatis R.C.* and written in German, in which the mysterious confraternity of the Rosy Cross reveals its own existence and affords some information on its history and on its mythical founder, Christian Rosencreutz, who supposedly lived in the fifteenth century and learned secret revelations from Arab and Jewish scholars in the course of his wanderings in the Orient. In 1615, a second manifesto appeared, in Latin, the *Confessio fraternitatis Roseae crucis, Ad eruditos Europae.* The first manifesto expressed the hope that in Europe a society could arise that would possess gold, silver, and precious stones in abundance and distribute them among kings to satisfy their needs and legitimate aspirations, a society that would educate rulers, teaching them everything God permits mankind to know and supporting them with wise counsel.

Among their alchemical metaphors and more or less messianic invocations, both manifestos insist on the secret nature of the confraternity and on the anonymity of its members ("our edifice—if

even one hundred thousand people had seen it close—will be for-
ever intangible, indestructible, and hidden from the wicked
world"). Whence the final appeal of the *Fama* may seem the more
ambiguous, addressed to all the learned of Europe and urging them
to communicate with the authors of the manifesto: "Even if for
now we have not revealed our names, nor the occasion when we
shall meet, still we shall come without doubt to know the opinion
of all, in whatever language it be expressed; and anyone who sends
us his name will be able to confer with one of us in person or, if
there were some impediment, in writing."

Almost immediately, from every part of Europe, appeals to the
Rosicrucians began to be written. No one asserted a knowledge of
the Rosicrucians, no one claimed to be a Rosicrucian; all sought
somehow to suggest that they were in absolute agreement with the
program. Though the Rosicrucians were not to be found, letters to
them came from Julius Sperber, Robert Fludd, and Michael Maier,
who in his *Themis aurea* (1618) insisted that the confraternity really
did exist, even though the author admitted he was too humble a
person ever to have been a member of it. But, as Frances Yates observes in her *Rosicrucian Enlightenment*, the habitual behavior of the
Rosicrucian writers is to affirm not only that they are not Rosicrucians but that they have never encountered a single member of
the confraternity.[7] Johann Valentin Andrae and all his Tübingen cir-
cle of friends, who were immediately suspected of being the authors of the manifestos, spent their lives either denying the fact or
playing it down, passing it off as a literary game, a youthful error. For
that matter, not only are there no historical proofs of the existence
of the Rosicrucians, but by definition none can exist. Even today,
the official documents of the AMORC (Anticus and Mysticus Ordo
Rosae Crucis), whose temple, rich in Egyptian iconography, can be
visited at San José, California, assert that the original texts legit-
imizing the order surely exist, but for obvious reasons they will remain secret, sealed in inaccessible archives.

But we are not interested so much in today's Rosicrucians, who
belong to folklore, as in those who belong to history. From the

first appearance of the two manifestos, other pamphlets, in opposition, appeared, attacking the confraternity with various accusations, especially of falsehood and charlatanism. In 1623 anonymous manifestos circulated in Paris, announcing the arrival of the Rosicrucians in the French capital, and this announcement unleashed fierce polemics, in both Catholic and libertine circles. The same year an anonymous publication, *Effroyables pactions faites entre le diable et les prétendus invisibles*, expressed the common notion that the Rosicrucians were Satan worshipers. Even Descartes, after having tried—according to rumor—to approach them (obviously without success) during a journey in Germany, was suspected on his return to Paris of belonging to the confraternity. He saved the situation with a stroke of genius: according to legend the Rosicrucians were invisible, so he displayed himself on many public occasions and thus quashed the rumor, as Baillet recounts in his *Vie de Monsieur Descartes* (1691). In 1623 a certain Neuhaus published, first in German and then in French, an *Avertissement pieux et utile des frères de la Rosée-Croix*, in which he pondered their existence and who they were and where they had found their name and to what purpose they came out in public. He concluded with the extraordinary argument that "inasmuch as they alter and anagram their names, and conceal their ages, and arrive without making themselves known, there is no Logic that can deny that they necessarily exist." Apparently, any appeal to the spiritual reform of humanity was enough to prompt the most paradoxical reactions, as if all were waiting for a decisive event.

Jorge Luis Borges, in his "Tlön, Uqbar, Orbis Tertius," tells of an improbable country, described by an inaccessible encyclopedia. It emerges, from other vague evidence found in reciprocally plagiarized texts, that in fact an entire planet is involved, "with its architecture and its playing cards, its mythological terrors and the sound of its dialects, its emperors and its oceans, its minerals, its birds, and its fishes, its algebra and its fire, its theological and metaphysical arguments." This planet is begotten by "a secret society of astronomers, biologists, engineers, metaphysicians, poets, chemists, mathematicians, moralists, painters and geomtricians, all under the supervision of an unknown genius."[8]

We are in the presence of a typical Borges invention: the invention of an invention. Still Borges readers know that Borges has never invented anything: his most paradoxical stories are born from a rereading of history. In fact, at one point Borges says that one of his sources is a work of Johann Valentin Andrae (but Borges draws the information secondhand, from De Quincey), who "described the imaginary community of Rosae Crucis—the community that was later founded by others in imitation of the one he had preconceived" (20).

In fact, the Rosicrucian story produced historical developments of no small significance. The symbolic masonry, a transformation of the operative masonry represented by actual confraternities of artisans that had retained over centuries terminology and ceremonies of the ancient builders of cathedrals, was born in the eighteenth century, thanks to certain English gentlemen. With the Constitutions of Anderson, the symbolic masonry tried to become legitimate by insisting on the antiquity of its origins, which the Masons dated back to the builders of the Temple of Solomon. In subsequent years, through the work of Ramsay, from whom the so-called Scottish Rite derived, the myth of the origins is enriched by the imagined relationship between the builders of the Temple and the Templars, whose secret tradition was to arrive at modern masonry through the mediation of the confraternity of the Rosicrucians.

The Rosicrucian theme with its mystical and occultist elements was used by the original Freemasons to compete with the throne and the altar, but at the beginning of the nineteenth century the Rosicrucian and Templar myth was revived in defense of throne and altar, to combat the spirit of the Enlightenment.

The myth of the secret societies and the existence of Superior Unknowns who directed the fate of the world already were debated before the French Revolution. In 1789 the marquis de Luchet (in his *Essai sur la secte des illuminés*) warned that "amid the deepest shadows a society has been formed of new beings who know one another without ever having seen one another. . . . This society takes from the Jesuit rule blind obedience; from the masonry, the tests and the external ceremonies; from the Templars, the underground evocations and the incredible audacity."

Between 1797 and 1798, in reaction to the French Revolution, the abbé Barruel wrote his *Mémoires pour servir à l'histoire du jacobinisme*, apparently a work of history, though it can be read as a serialized novel. After their destruction by Philip the Fair, the Templars transformed themselves into a secret society to destroy the monarchy and the papacy. In the eighteenth century they took over the Masons and created a kind of academy whose diabolical members were Voltaire, Turgot, Condorcet, Diderot, and d'Alembert. From this little group originated the Jacobins, themselves controlled by an even more secret society, that of the Illuminati of Bavaria, regicides by vocation. The French Revolution was the final outcome of this conspiracy. Never mind that there were profound differences between secular and enlightened masonry and the masonry of the "Illuminati," which was occultist and Templar; never mind that the myth of the Templars had already been exploded by a fellow traveler, who then traveled in a different direction, namely, Joseph de Maistre. The story was too fascinating to be derailed by fact.

Barruel's book contained no reference to the Jews. But in 1806 Barruel received a letter from a Captain Simonini, who reminded him how both Mani and the Old Man of the Mountain of Moslem memory (with whom the Templars had been suspected of connivance) were Jews (and you see that here the game of occult ancestries becomes head-spinning). The masonry had been founded by the Jews, who had infiltrated all the secret societies.

Barruel did not openly refer to this rumor, which for that matter produced no interesting effects until the middle of the century, when the Jesuits began to worry about the anticlerical inspirers of the Risorgimento, men like Garibaldi, affiliated with the masonry. The idea of demonstrating that the Carbonari were emissaries of a Jewish-masonic plot seemed polemically fertile.

The same anticlericals, still in the nineteenth century, tried to defame the Jesuits, demonstrating that they did nothing but conspire against the welfare of humanity. It was less the few "serious" writers (from Michelet and Quinet to Garibaldi and Gioberti) who made the subject popular than the novelist Eugène Sue. In his *Juif errant*, the wicked Monsieur Rodin, the quintessence of Jesuitical conspiracy, clearly appears as a replica of the Higher Unknowns of both masonic and clerical memory. Monsieur Rodin returns in Sue's last novel, *Les Mystères du peuple*, in which the evil Jesuit plot is revealed down to the least detail. Rodolphe de Gerolstein, who has migrated into this novel from *Les Mystères de Paris*, denounces the Jesuits' plan, revealing "with what shrewdness this infernal plot was organized, what frightful disasters, what horrendous enslavement, what future despotism it would mean for Europe."

After the appearance of Sue's novels, in 1864 Maurice Joly wrote a pamphlet, inspired by liberalism, against Napoleon III, in which Machiavelli, who represents the dictator's cynicism, talks with Montesquieu. The Jesuit plot described by Sue is then attributed by Joly to Napoleon III.

In 1868 Hermann Goedsche, who had already published some clearly slanderous opuscules, wrote a popular novel, *Biarritz*, under the psuedonym of Sir John Retcliffe, in which he described an occult ritual in the cemetery of Prague. Goedsche simply copied a scene from Dumas's *Giuseppe Balsamo* (1849), which described an encounter between Cagliostro, head of the Higher Unknowns, and other Illuminati, when, together, they plot the affair of the queen's necklace. But instead of Cagliostro and Co., Goedsche brings on the representatives of the twelve tribes of Israel, who meet to prepare the conquest of the world. Five years later, the same story appeared in a Russian pamphlet (the title of which translates as "The Jews, Masters of the World") as if it were factual reportage. In 1881 *Le Contemporain* republished the story, asserting that it came from an unimpeachable source, the English diplomat Sir John Readcliff. In 1806 François Bournand again used the speech of the Grand Rabbi (this time he is called John Readclif) in his book *Les Juifs, nos contemporains*. From this point on, the masonic meeting invented by Dumas, blended with the Jesuit plan invented by Sue and attributed by Joly to Napoleon III, becomes the authentic speech of the Grand Rabbi and reappears in various forms and various places.

Now Pyotr Ivanovich Rachovskij appears on the stage, a Russian formerly suspected of contacts with revolutionary groups and nihilists and later (duly repentant) a friend of the Black Centuria, an extreme-right terrorist organization. First informer and then chief of the czarist political police, the Okhrana, Rachovskij, to help his political protector Count Sergej Witte, who is worried about a rival, Elie de Cyon, had had Cyon's house searched and had found a pamphlet in which Cyon had copied Joly's text against Napoleon III but ascribing Machiavelli's ideas to Witte. Fiercely anti-Semitic (these events took place at the time of the Dreyfus case), Rachovskij took the text, deleted every reference to Witte, and attributed those ideas to the Jews. A man cannot bear the name of Cyon (even with a *c*) without suggesting a Jewish conspiracy.

The text revised by Rachovskij probably represented the primary source of the *Protocols of the Elders of Zion*. Rachovskij's version reveals its novelistic source because it is scarcely credible, except in a novel of Sue, that the bad guys should express so openly, so shamelessly, their evil plans. The Elders freely declare that they possess "boundless ambition, devouring greed, a pitiless desire for vengeance and an intense hatred." They want to abolish freedom of the press, but they encourage libertarianism. They criticize liberalism but support the idea of capitalist multinationals. To provoke revolution in every country they mean to exacerbate social inequality. They want to build subways the better to mine the big cities. They want to abolish study of the classics and ancient history; they mean to encourage sport and visual communication in order to make the working class stupid.

It is easy to recognize the *Protocols* as stemming from a document produced in nineteenth century France: they are filled with references to problems of French society at the time. But it is also easy to recognize, among the sources, many well-known popular novels. Alas, the story—once again—was so convincingly narrated that it was easy to take it seriously.

The rest of this story is history. An itinerant Russian monk, Sergej Nilus, obsessed by the idea of the Antichrist, published, in order to foster his own "Rasputinian" ambitions, the text of the *Protocols*, with his commentary. After that the text traveled throughout Europe and even fell into the hands of Hitler.[9]

Falsehood and Verisimilitude

What do all the stories I have mentioned have in common? And what made them so persuasive and credible?

The Donation of Constantine was probably not created as an explicit fake but as a rhetorical exercise, which only later began to be taken seriously. The Rosicrucian manifestos were, at least according to their supposed authors, an erudite game, if not a joke, then a literary exercise that could be ascribed to the utopist genre. The letter of Prester John was certainly a deliberate fake, but just as certainly it was not meant to produce the effects it produced. Cosmas Indicopleustes committed the sin of fundamentalism, a forgivable weakness given the period in which he lived, but, as we have seen, no one really took him seriously, and his text was maliciously exhumed and called authoritative only after more than a thousand years. The *Protocols* came into existence virtually on their own, through an agglomeration of novel-like themes that gradually kindled the imagination of a few fanatics and were slowly transformed.

And yet each of these stories had a virtue: as narratives, they seemed plausible, more than everyday or historical reality, which is far more complex and less credible. The stories seemed to explain something that was otherwise hard to understand.

We will take another look at the story of Ptolemy. Today we know that the Ptolemaic hypothesis was scientifically false. And yet, if our knowledge is by now Copernican, our perception is still

Ptolemaic: we not only see the sun rise in the east and travel through the arc of the day, but we behave as if the sun turns and we remain immobile. And we say, "the sun rises," "the sun is high in the sky," "it sinks," "it sets." Even your astronomy professors speak Ptolemaically.

Why should the tale of the Donation of Constantine have been rejected? It guaranteed a continuity of power after the fall of the empire, it perpetuated an idea of Latinity, it indicated a guide, a reference point amid the flames of the massacres perpetrated by the many suitors disputing the nuptial bed of Europa.

Why refuse the story of Cosmas? In other respects he had been an alert traveler, a diligent collector of geographical and historical curiosities, and furthermore his flat-earth theory—at least from a narrative point of view—displayed some verisimilitude: the earth was a great rectangle bounded by four immense walls that supported two layers of heavenly vault; on the first the stars shone and, in the cavity between the two, the inner ceiling, lived the Blest; astronomical phenomena were explained by the presence of a very high mountain to the north that, hiding the sun, created night and, coming between sun and light, produced eclipses.

Why reject the story of the Rosicrucians, when it satisfied an expectation of religious harmony? And why reject the story of the *Protocols*, if they could explain so many historic events by the myth of the conspiracy? Karl Popper has reminded us that the social theory of conspiracy is like the one we find in Homer. Homer conceived the power of the gods in such a way that everything taking place on the plain before Troy represented only a reflection of the countless conspiracies devised on Olympus. The social theory of conspiracy, Popper says, is a consequence of the end of God as a reference point and of the consequent question, Who is there in his place? This place is now occupied by various men and powerful, sinister groups that can be blamed for having organized the Great Depression and all the evils we suffer.[10]

Why consider absurd the belief in plots and conspiracies when today they are still used to explain the failure of our own actions or the reason that events have taken a different turn from that desired?

False tales are, first of all, tales, and tales, like myths, are always persuasive. And we could mention many, many other false tales, for example, the myth of the Terra Australis, that immense continent that supposedly extended all along the polar cap and subtropical Antarctica. The firm belief in the existence of this land (affirmed by countless maps showing the globe encircled, to the south, by a broad terrestrial band), drove navigators from various nations for at least three centuries to try to explore the south seas and even the Antarctic.

What can be said of the idea of Eldorado and the fountain of youth, which led mad, brave heroes to explore the two Americas? Or the stimulus given to nascent chemistry by hallucinations inspired by the phantom of the philosopher's stone? And what about the tale of Phlogiston, the tale of cosmic ether?

Let us forget for a moment that some of these false tales produced positive effects, while others produced horror and shame. All created something, for better or worse. Nothing in their success is inexplicable. What represents a problem is rather the way they managed to replace other tales that today we consider true. Some years ago, in an essay of mine on fakes and counterfeits, I concluded that although instruments, whether empirical or conjectural, exist to prove that some object is false, every decision in the matter presupposes the existence of an original, authentic and true, to which the fake is compared. The truly genuine problem thus does not consist of proving something false but in proving that the authentic object is authentic.

And yet this obvious consideration must not lead us to the conclusion that a criterion of truth does not exist and that tales now called false and tales that today we believe true are equivalent because both belong to the genre of narrative fiction. There exists a process of verification that is based on slow, collective, public performance by what Charles Sanders Peirce called "the Community." It is thanks to human faith in the work of this community that we can say, with some serenity, that the Donation of Constantine was false, that the earth turns around the sun, and that Saint Thomas at least knew the planet is round. At most, recognizing that our history was inspired by many tales we now recognize as false should make us alert, ready to call constantly into question the very tales we believe true, because the criterion of the wisdom of the community is based on constant awareness of the fallibility of our learning.

Some years ago in France a book by Jean-François Gautier appeared, entitled *L'Univers existe-t-il?* (Does the universe exist?).[11] Good question. What if the universe were a concept like cosmic ether, or phlogiston, or the conspiracy of the Elders of Zion?

Philosophically, Gautier's arguments make sense. The idea of the universe, as the totality of the cosmos, is one that comes from the most ancient cosmographies, cosmologies, and cosmogonies. But can one describe, as if seeing it from above, something within which we are contained, of which we are part, and from which we cannot exit? Can there be a descriptive geometry of the universe when there is no space outside it on which to project it? Can we talk about the beginning of the universe, when a temporal notion such as "beginning" must refer to the parameter of a clock, while the universe must be the clock of itself and cannot be referred to anything that is external to it? Can we say, as Eddington does, that a hundred billion stars constitute a galaxy and a hundred billion galaxies constitute the universe, when, as Gautier observes, while a galaxy is an observable object, the universe is not, and therefore we would be establishing an improper analogy between two incommensurable objects? Can we postulate the universe and then study with empirical instruments this postulate as if it were an object? Can a singular object exist (surely the most singular of all) that has as its characteristic that of being only a law? And what if the story of the big bang were a tale as fantastic as the gnostic account that insisted the universe was generated by the lapsus of a clumsy demiurge? Basically, this criticism of the notion of the universe reiterates Kant's criticism of the notion of the world.

At a certain historical moment, some people found the suspicion that the sun did not revolve around the earth just as crazy and deplorable as the suspicion that the universe does not exist. So we would be wise to keep an open, fresh mind against the moment when the community of scientists decrees that the idea of the universe has been an illusion, just like the flat earth and the Rosicrucians.

After all, the cultivated person's first duty is to be always prepared to rewrite the encyclopedia.

2 | LANGUAGES IN PARADISE

This story starts in the Garden of Eden, where Adam speaks with God, and ends at the Heaven of the Fixed Stars, where Dante Alighieri (*Paradise* xxvi) meets Adam and speaks with him.

Afterward, language will play a lesser role in Dante's travels. Even though he still talks with Saint Peter, Beatrice, or Saint Bernard, he is coming closer and closer to the site of the highest angelical hierarchies, and, as everybody knows, angels do not speak because they understand each other through a sort of instantaneous mental reading, and they know everything they are allowed to know (according to their rank) not by any linguistic intercourse but by watching the Divine Mind. At this point, as Dante says in the final canto of the *Divine Comedy*, language is unable to express what he sees: *A l'alta fantasia qui mancò possa*—high fantasy lost power and here broke off.

Nevertheless, my story has an advantage over many others: it can begin at the very Beginning.

Beréshit, God spoke and said, "Let there be light." In this way, He created both Heaven and Earth; for, with the utterance of the Divine Word, "there was light" (Genesis 1:3, 4). Thus Creation itself arose through an act of speech; it was only by giving things their names that God created them and gave them an ontological status: "And God called the light Day and the darkness he called Night . . . . And God called the firmament Heaven" (1:5, 8). In Genesis 2:16–17, the Lord speaks to man for the first time, putting at his disposal everything in the earthly paradise, commanding him, however, not to eat of the fruit of the tree of good and evil. We are not told in what language God spoke to Adam. Tradition imagined it as a sort of language of interior illumination, in which God, as in other episodes of the Bible, expressed himself by thunderclaps and lightning. If we are to understand it in this way, we must conceive of a language that, although not translatable into any known idiom, is still, through special grace or disposition, comprehensible to its hearer.

It is at this point, and only at this point (2:19), that "out of the ground the Lord God formed every beast of the field, and every fowl of the air; and brought *them* unto Adam to see what he would call them." The interpretation of this passage is an extremely delicate matter. Clearly we are here in the presence of a motif, common to other religions and mythologies: that of the Nomothete, the Name Giver, the creator of language. Yet it is not at all clear on what basis Adam actually chose the names he gave to the animals. The version in the Vulgate, the source for European culture's understanding of the passage, does little to resolve this mystery. The Vulgate has Adam call the various animals *nominibus suis*, which we can translate only as "by their own names." The King James version does not help us anymore: "Whatsoever Adam called every living creature, that *was* the name thereof" (Genesis 2:19). Luther's German translation puts it: "Denn wie der Mensch allerlei lebendige Tiere nennen würde so solten sie heissen. Und der Mensch gab einem jeglichen Vieh und Vogel unter dem Himmel und Tier auf dem Felde seinen Namen."

Thus Adam might have called the animals "by their own names" in two senses. Either he gave them the names that, by some extralinguistic right, were already *due* them, or he gave them those names we still use on the basis of a convention initiated by Adam. In other words, the names Adam gave the animals are either the names that each animal intrinsically *ought* to have been given or simply the names that the Name Giver arbitrarily and *ad placitum* decided to give them.

From this difficulty, we pass to Genesis 2:23. Here Adam sees Eve for the first time, and here, for the first time, the reader hears Adam's actual words. In the King James version, Adam is quoted as saying: "This *is* now bone of my bones, and flesh of my flesh: she shall be called Woman" (in the Vulgate the name is *virago*, a translation from the Hebrew *ishha*, the feminine of *ish*, "man"). If we take Adam's use of *virago* together with the fact that, in Genesis 3:20, he calls his wife Eve, meaning "life," because "she was the mother of all living," it is evident that we are dealing with names that are not arbitrary but rather—at least etymologically—"right."

The linguistic theme is taken up once more, this time in a very explicit fashion, in Genesis 11:1. We are told that after the Flood, "the whole earth was of one language, and of one speech." Yet man in his vanity conceived a desire to rival the Lord and thus to erect a tower that would reach up to the heavens. The Lord punishes humanity's pride and puts a stop to the construction of the tower: "Go to, let us go down, and there confound their language, that they may not understand one another's speech. . . . Therefore is the name of it called Babel; because the Lord did there confound the language of all the earth; and from thence did the Lord scatter them abroad upon the face of the earth" (11:7–9). In the opinion of various Arab authors, the confusion was due to the trauma induced by the sight, no doubt terrifying, of the collapse of the tower. This really changes nothing: the biblical story, as well as the partially divergent accounts of other mythologies, simply serve to establish the fact that different languages exist in the world.

Told in this way, however, the story is still incomplete. We have left out Genesis 10. Here, speaking of the dispersal of the sons of Noah after the Flood, the text states of the sons of Japheth that, "By these [sons] were the isles of the Gentiles divided in their lands; every one after his tongue, after their families, in their nations" (10:5). This idea is repeated in similar words for the sons of Ham (10:20) and of Shem (10:31). How are we meant to interpret this evident plurality of languages prior to Babel? The account presented in Genesis 11 is dramatic, able to inspire visual representations, as is shown by the subsequent iconographic tradition. The account in Genesis 10 is, by contrast, less theatrical. It is obvious that tradition focused on the story in which the existence of a plurality of tongues was understood as the tragic consequence of the confusion after Babel and the result of a divine malediction. Where it was not neglected entirely, Genesis 10 was reduced to a sort of footnote, a provincial episode recounting the diffusion of tribal dialects not the multiplication of tongues.

Thus Genesis 11 seems to possess a clear and unequivocal meaning: first there was one language, and then there were—depending on which tradition we follow—seventy or seventy-two. It is this story that served as point of departure for any number of dreams of restoring the language of Adam. Genesis 10, however, has continued to lurk in the background with all its explosive potential still intact, so that at a certain moment somebody suspected that the original Hebrew spoken by Adam was already lost after Noah.

Greek and Roman cultures were not worried about the multiplicity of languages. This indifference was primarily practical and political: Greek *koiné* first and imperial Latin later ensured a satisfactory universal system of communication from the Mediterranean basin to the British Isles. Further, the two peoples that had invented the language of law identified the structures of their languages with the structures of human reason: Greek man spoke the Language; the rest were Barbarians, that is, in etymological terms, those who stutter, who have no language.

Of course the philosophers knew that even barbarians speak and think. Even so Greek culture did not distinguish between linguistic and mental structures: Aristotle constructed his list of categories setting out from the structures of Greek grammar. Later the Stoics would recognize that although the barbarians used different words they had the same concepts in mind. Nevertheless, the Greek culture continued to think of a universality of the Logos beyond the difference between the various languages.

Conversely, the ancient Greeks debated a problem that Genesis left unsolved, that is, the problem of the relationship between names and things. Plato in the *Cratylus* discusses the problem of whether words have their source in nature, by direct imitation of things, or in law, by convention. He does not make a definitive choice; indeed, he suggests a third option, that language must reflect the order of ideas. European culture was for a long time directly influenced by Aristotle's solution: the sounds of the voice are conventional symbols that express a passion of the soul, even though this passion of the soul arises spontaneously as the image of the thing that exists.

When Christianity became a state religion, it was expressed in the Greek of the patristic East and further in the Western Latin. After St. Jerome translated the Old Testament in the fourth century, the need to know Hebrew as a sacred language grew weaker. A typical example of this cultural lack is given by St. Augustine, a man of vast culture and the most important exponent of Christian thought at the end of the empire. Obviously, according to Augustine, the Christian revelation is founded on an Old Testament written in Hebrew and a New Testament known as a Greek text. St. Augustine, however, knew no Hebrew, and his knowledge of Greek was, to say the least, patchy. Hence a somewhat paradoxical situation ensues: the man who set himself the task of interpreting the Scripture in order to discover the true meaning of the Divine Word could read it only in Latin translations. The notion that he ought to consult the Hebrew original never really seems to have entered Augustine's mind. He did not entirely trust the Jews, nurturing a suspicion that, in their versions, they might have erased all references to the coming of Christ. The only critical procedure he would allow was a comparison of translations in order to find the most likely version. Thus St. Augustine, though the father of hermeneutics, was certainly not destined to become the father of Semitic philology.

Nevertheless, for Augustine, as for nearly all the early Fathers, Hebrew certainly was the primordial language. It was the language spoken before Babel, and after the confusion, it still remained the tongue of the chosen people. Still, Augustine gave no sign of wanting to recover its use. He was at home in Latin, by now the language of the Church and of theology. Some centuries later, Isidore of Seville found it easy to assume that, in any case, there were three sacred languages—Hebrew, Greek, and Latin— because these were the three languages that appeared written above the cross (*Etymologiarum* ix, i). With this conclusion, the task of determining the language in which the Lord said "Fiat lux" became more arduous.

If anything, the Fathers were concerned about another linguistic puzzle: the Bible clearly states that God brought before Adam all the beasts of the field and all the fowl of the air. What about fish? Did Adam name the fish? Perhaps it seemed difficult (even for God) to drag them all up from the depth of the seas and parade them in the garden of Eden. We may think this a slight matter, yet the question, whose last trace is still to be found in theological discussions of the eighteenth century, was never satisfactorily resolved, even though Augustine had suggested that the fish were named one at a time, step by step, as they were discovered (*De Genesi ad litteram libri duodecim* XII, 20).

Between the fall of the Roman Empire and the early Middle Ages, when Europe had still to emerge, new languages came slowly into being. It has been calculated that toward the end of the fifth century people no longer spoke Latin but Gallo-Romanic, Italico-Romanic, or Hispano-Romanic. While intellectuals continued to write Latin, bastardizing it ever further, they heard around them local dialects in which survivals of languages spoken before Roman civilization crossed with new roots brought by the barbarian invaders.

It is in the seventh century, before any known document written in Romance or Germanic languages, that the first reference to our theme appears. It is contained in an attempt, on the part of some Irish grammarians, to defend spoken Gaelic over learned Latin. In a work titled *Auracepit na n-Éces* (The precepts of the poets), the Irish grammarians refer to the structural material of the Tower of Babel as follows: "Others affirm that in the tower there were only nine materials and that these were clay and water, wool and blood, wood and lime, pitch, linen, and bitumen....These represent noun, pronoun, verb, adverb, participle, conjunction, preposition, interjection." Thus the Gaelic language constituted the first and only instance of a language that overcame the confusion of tongues. It was the first language created after the fall of the tower by the seventy-two wise men of the school of Fenius. They were said to have implemented a sort of (to speak in computer jargon) cut-and-paste operation on all the languages born after the dispersion. All that was best in each language, all there was that was grand or beautiful, was cut out and retained in Irish. Wherever there was something that had no name in any other language, a name for it was made up in Irish. This firstborn and consequently supernatural language retained traces of its original isomorphism with the created world. As long as the proper order of its elements was respected, this ensured a sort of natural link between names and things.

Why did such a document appear at this particular moment? A quick look at the iconographic history increases our curiosity. There are no known representations of the Tower of Babel before the Cotton Bible (fifth or sixth century). It next appears in a manuscript perhaps from the end of the tenth century and then on a relief from the cathedral of Salerno from the eleventh century. After this, however, there is a flood of towers. It is a flood, moreover, that has its counterpart in a vast deluge of theoretical speculation about the confusion of tongues. It was only at this point that the story of the confusion came to be perceived not merely as an example of how divine justice humbled man's pride but as an account of a historical (or metahistorical) event. It was now the story of how a real wound had been inflicted on mankind, a wound that might, in some way, be healed.

It thus happens that as soon as Europe was born as a bunch of peoples speaking different tongues, European culture reacted by feeling such an event not as a beginning but as the end of a lost harmony, a new Babel-like disaster, so that a remedy for linguistic confusion needed to be sought. I have already told the story of this quest.[1] It is a quest that took two different paths: on one hand, people (from Raymond Lully to Leibniz and further) looked ahead, aiming to fabricate a rational language possessing the perfection of the lost speech of Eden; on the other hand, people tried to rediscover the lost language spoken by Adam.

Two different paths, but they did not remain strictly separate. Even when thinkers dreamed of a new language of universal reason, the model for that language was based on a theoretical idea of the possible aboriginal Hebrew of Adam. Since the story (which lasted for at least one thousand years and under certain points of view has not yet finished) has to be told here through several shortcuts, let me consider the case of Dante Alighieri.

Between 1303 and 1305, thus before finishing the *Divine Comedy* and certainly before writing Canto 26 of the *Paradise* (of which I must speak later), Dante Alighieri wrote his *De Vulgari Eloquentia.* Though it appears to be a doctrinal treatise, it is a self-commentary in which the author tends to analyze his own methods of artistic production, which he implicitly identifies as the exemplar of every poetic discourse.

Dante's text opens with an observation that, obvious though it may be, is still fundamental for us: there are a multitude of vulgar tongues, and all of them are natural languages, opposed to Latin, which is (or which had become by Dante's time) a universal but artificial grammar.

Before the blasphemy of Babel, mankind had known but one language, a perfect language, a language spoken by Adam and his posterity. The plurality of tongues arose as the consequence of the *confusio linguarum.* Revealing a knowledge of comparative linguistics exceptional for his time, Dante sought to demonstrate how this fragmentation had actually taken place. First, languages split up into the various zones of the world and, using the vernacular word for *yes* as a measuring rod, the languages (within what we today call the Romance area) further split into the *oc*, *oil*, and *si* groups. Then, even these vernacular languages further fragmented into a welter of local dialects, some of which might, as in Bologna, even vary from one part of a city to another. All these divisions had occurred, Dante observed, because man is—by custom, habit, language, and according to the differences in time and space—a changeable animal.

Dante's project was to discover one language, more decorous and illustrious than the others, which had to become the language of his own poetry. To create such a language Dante had to take the various vernaculars in turn and subject each to a severe critical analysis. Examining the work of the best Italian poets and assuming that each in his own way had always gone beyond the local dialect, Dante wanted to create a vernacular that might be more *illustris* ("illustrious," in the sense of "shining with light"), useful as guiding rule, worthy of being spoken in the royal palace of the national king, if the Italians were ever to obtain one), and worthy to be a language of government, of courts of law, and of wisdom. Such a vernacular belonged to every city in Italy and yet to none. It existed only as an ideal form, approached by the best poets, and it was according to this ideal form that all the vulgar dialects had to be judged.

The second, and uncompleted, part of *De Vulgari Eloquentia* sketches out the rules of composition for the one and only vernacular to which the term *illustrious* might truly apply: the poetic language of which Dante considered himself to be the founder. Opposing this language to all other languages of the confusion, Dante proclaimed it as the one that had restored that primordial affinity between words and objects that had been the hallmark of the language of Adam.

An apology for the vernacular, *De Vulgari Eloquentia* is written in Latin. As a poet, Dante wrote in Italian; as a philosopher, he stuck to the language of theology and law. Dante defines a vernacular as the speech that an infant learns as it first begins to articulate, imitating the sounds made to it by its nurse, before knowing any rule. The same was not true of that *locutio secundaria*, called "grammar" by the Romans. Grammar meant a rule-governed language, one, moreover, that could be mastered only after long study to acquire the *habitus*. Considering that in the vocabulary of the Schoolmen *habitus* was a virtue, a capacity to do some specific thing, a present-day reader might take Dante merely to be distinguishing between the instinctive ability to express oneself in language (performance) and grammatical competence. It is clear, however, that by *grammar* Dante meant scholastic Latin, the only language whose rules were taught in school during this period. In this sense Latin was an *artificial* idiom; it was, moreover, an idiom that was "perpetual and incorruptible," having been ossified into the international language of church and university through a system of rules established by grammarians from Servius,between the fourth and fifth centuries, to Priscian, between the fifth and sixth, when Latin had ceased to be the living language of the Romans.

Having clarified this distinction between a primary and a secondary language, Dante went on to proclaim in no uncertain terms that, of the two, it was the first, the vernacular, that was the more noble. Vernaculars were the first languages of mankind, "though divided by different words and accents" (I, i, 4).

This choice confronted Dante, however, with a double predicament. First, although assuming that the most noble language must be natural, the fact that natural languages were split into a multiplicity of dialects suggested that they were not natural but conventional. Second, a vulgar tongue is the language spoken by everyone (by *vulgus*, or common people). But in *De Vulgari Eloquentia* Dante insists on the variety of the languages of the world. How could he reconcile the idea that languages are many with the idea that the vernacular was *the* natural language for the whole human race?

One way to escape this double predicament would be to interpret Dante's argument to mean that our ability to learn different natural languages (according to our place of birth or our first linguistic training) depends on our native faculty for languages. This is certainly an innate faculty that manifests itself in different linguistic forms, that is, in our ability to speak different natural languages.

Such a reading would be legitimated by a number of Dante's assertions concerning our faculty to learn a mother tongue; this faculty is natural, it exists in all peoples despite differences of word and accent, and it is not associated with any specific language. It is a general faculty, possessed by man as a species, for "only man is able to speak" (I, ii, 1). The ability to speak is thus a specific trait of man, one that is not possessed by angels, or beasts, or demons. Speaking involves an ability to externalize our particular thoughts; angels, on the contrary, have an "ineffable intellectual capacity" (I, ii, 3): they either understand the thoughts of others, or they can read them in the divine mind. Animals, for their part, lack individual feelings, possessing only "specific" passions (I, ii, 5). Consequently, each knows its own feelings and may recognize feelings when displayed by animals of the same species, having no need to understand the feelings of other species. Finally, each demon immediately recognizes the depths of perfidy in others. (By the way, when Dante decides to make his demons talk in the *Divine Comedy*, they use a not-quite-human speech: the celebrated diabolical expression in *Inferno* VII, 1, "Papé Satàn, papé Satàn aleppe," is curiously reminiscent of another expression, "Raphèl may amècche zabì almì" (*Inferno* XXXI, 67), the fatal words, spoken by Nimrod, that set off the catastrophe of Babel. Even the devils thus speak the language of the confusion. While the first expression seems a mixture of Greek and Semitic words, the second looks like a caricature of Hebrew. This point is worthy of note because it shows Dante did not know Hebrew but had a vague idea of how Hebrew could sound, and this point will prove of some interest for my further hypotheses).

In any case, men are neither angels nor demons, are guided by reason, and need some faculty that can allow them to externalize the contents of their intellect in outward signs (even though, accepting the Aristotelian doctrine, Dante accepts the idea that the relation between signs and thoughts and the things they signify is conventional and changes from language to language).

This tendency to associate sound with thoughts is not to be identified with the existing natural languages; it is a permanent and immutable trait of the human species, whereas natural languages are historically subject to variation and are capable of developing over the course of time, enriching themselves independently of the will of any single speaker. Dante was also aware that a natural language can be enriched through the creativity of single individuals, for the illustrious vernacular that he intended to shape was to be the product of just such an individual creative effort. Yet it seemed that between the faculty of language and the natural languages that are the ultimate result, Dante wished to posit an intermediate stage. We can see this better by looking at Dante's treatment of the story of Adam.

In referring to his conception of the vernacular, Dante uses terms such as *vulgaris eloquentia, locutio vulgarium gentium,* and *vulgaris locutio,* reserving the term *locutio secundaria* for grammar. We can probably take *eloquentia* generically to mean "the ability to speak fluently." Still, the text contains a series of distinctions, and these are probably not casual. In certain instances, Dante speaks of *locutio,* in others of *ydioma, lingua,* or *loquela.* He uses the term *ydioma* whenever he refers to the Hebrew language and when he expresses his notion of the branching-off of the various languages of the world. In I, vi, 6–7, speaking of the confusion after Babel, Dante used the term *loquela.* In this same context, however, he uses *ydioma* for the languages of the confusion, as well as for the Hebrew language, which remained intact. He could speak of the *loquela* of the Genovese and the Tuscans while at the same time using *lingua* both for Hebrew and for the Italian vernacular dialects. It thus seems that the terms *ydioma, lingua,* and *loquela* are all to be understood as "tongue" or a given language in the modern, Saussurian sense of *langue.*

a singular fashion, suggesting that God was able to move the air in such a way that it resonated to form true words. Why did Dante find it necessary to propose such a cumbersome and apparently gratuitous reading? The answer seems to be that, as the first member of the only species that uses speech, Adam could conceive ideas only through hearing linguistic sounds. Moreover, as Dante also makes clear (I, v, 2), God wanted Adam to speak so that he could use the gift to glorify His name.

Dante must then ask in what idiom Adam spoke. He criticized those (the Florentines in particular) who believed their native language to be the best. There are a great many native languages, Dante commented, and many of these are better than the Italian vernaculars. He then affirmed that, along with the first soul, God created a *certam formam locutionis* (I, vi, 4).

This expression has produced hundreds of pages attempting to establish what that *forma locutionis* was. According to certain interpreters it meant "a given form of language," but such a translation would not explain why Dante, shortly thereafter, states that "it was therefore the Hebrew language [*ydioma*] that the lips of the first speaker forged [*fabricarunt*]" (I, vi, 7).

It is true that Dante specifies that he is speaking here of a form "in regard to the expressions that indicate things, as well as to the construction of these expressions and their grammatical endings," allowing the inference that, by *forma locutionis*, he wished to refer to a lexicon and a morphology and consequently to a given language. Nevertheless, translating *forma locutionis* as "language" would render the next passage difficult to understand:

Qua quidem forma omnis lingua loquentium uteretur, nisi culpa presumptionis humanae dissipata fuisset, ut inferius ostenderentur. Hac forma locutionis locutus est Adam: hac forma locutionis locuti sunt homines posteri ejus usque ad edificationem turris Babel, quae "turris confusionis" interpretatur: hanc formam locutionis hereditati sunt filii Heber, qui ab eo sunt dicti Hebrei. Hiis solis post confusionem remansit, ut Redemptor noster, qui ex illis oritus erat secundum humanitatem, non lingua confusionis sed gratie frueretur. Fuit ergo hebraicum ydioma illud quod primi locuentis labia fabricarunt. (I, vi, 45–61).

On one side, if Dante wishes to use *forma locutionis* here to refer to a given tongue, why, in observing that Jesus spoke Hebrew, does he once use *lingua* and once *ydioma* (and in recounting the story if the confusion—I, vi, 6—the term *loquela*) while *forma locutionis* is only used apropos of the divine gift? On the other side, if we understand *forma locutionis* as a faculty of language innate in all humans, it is difficult to explain why the sinners of Babel are said to have lost it, since *De Vulgari Eloquentia* repeatedly acknowledges the existence of languages born after Babel. In the light of this, let us try to give a translation of the passage:

> And it is precisely this *form* that all speakers would make use of in their *language* had it not been dismembered through the fault of human presumption, as I shall demonstrate below. By this *linguistic form* Adam spoke: by this *linguistic form* spoke all his descendants until the construction of the tower of Babel— which is interpreted as the "tower of confusion": this was the *linguistic form* that the sons of Eber, called Hebrews after him, inherited. It remained to them alone after the confusion, so that our Savior, who because of the human side of his nature had to be born of them, could use a *language* not of confusion but of grace. It was thus the Hebrew *tongue* that was constructed by the first being *endowed with speech*. (italics mine)

In this way, the *forma locutionis* was neither the Hebrew language nor the general faculty of language but a particular gift from God to Adam that was lost after Babel. It is the lost gift that Dante sought to recover through his theory of an illustrious vernacular.

One solution to the problem has been proposed by Maria Corti:[2] It is, by now, generally accepted that we cannot regard

Dante as simply an orthodox follower of the thought of St. Thomas Aquinas. According to circumstances, Dante used a variety of philosophical and theological sources; it is furthermore well established that he was influenced by various strands of that so-called radical Aristotelianism whose major representative was Siger of Brabant. Another important figure in radical Aristotelianism was Boethius of Dacia, who, like Siger, suffered the condemnation of the bishop of Paris in 1277. Boethius was a member of a group of grammarians called Modistae and the author of a treatise, *De modis significandi*, that—according to Corti—influenced Dante.

The Modist grammarians asserted the existence of linguistic universals, that is, of rules underlying the formation of any natural language. This may help clarify precisely what Dante meant by *forma locutionis*. In his *De modis*, Boethius of Dacia observed that it was possible to extract from all existing languages the rules of a universal grammar, distinct from either Greek or Latin grammar (*Quaestio* VI). The speculative grammar of the Modistae asserted a relation of specular correspondence among language, thought, and the nature of things. For them, it was a given that the *modi intelligendi* and consequently the *modi significandi* reflected the *modi essendi* of things themselves.

What God gave Adam, therefore, was neither the simple faculty of language nor yet a natural language; it was, in fact, a set of principles for a universal grammar. These principles acted as the formal cause of language.

Maria Corti's thesis has been vehemently contested by other scholars on the grounds that (1) there is no clear proof that Dante even knew the work of Boethius of Dacia and that (2) many of the linguistic notions that one finds in Dante were already circulating in the works of philosophers even before the thirteenth century (for instance, the idea that grammar has one and the same substance in all languages, even if there are variations on the surface, was already present in Roger Bacon). Yet this, if anything, constitutes proof that it was possible that Dante could have been thinking about universal grammar, and it is immaterial by whom he was directly inspired. (One can say that the *forma locutionis* given by God is a sort of innate mechanism, in the same terms as Chomsky's generative grammar. And not because Dante was Chomskian, but because Chomsky, who is assumed to have been inspired by the rationalist ideals of Descartes and sixteenth-century grammarians, did not note that his inspirers were in some way themselves inspired by the ideas of the medieval Modistae.)

It thus seems most likely that Dante believed that, at Babel, there had disappeared the perfect *forma locutionis* whose principles permitted the creation of languages capable of reflecting the true essence of things, languages, in other words, in which the *modi essendi* of things were identical with the *modi significandi*. The Hebrew of Eden was the perfect and unrepeatable example of such a language.

What was left after Babel? All that remained were shattered, imperfect *formae locutionis*, imperfect as the various vulgar Italian dialects whose defects and whose incapacity to express grand and profound thoughts Dante pitilessly analyzed.

Now we can begin to understand the nature of the illustrious vernacular that Dante hunts like a perfumed panther (I, xvi, 1). We catch glimpses of it, evanescent, in the works of the poets that Dante considers the most important, but the language still remains unformed and unregulated, its grammatical principles unarticulated. Confronted with the existing vernaculars, natural but not universal languages, and a grammar that was universal but artificial, Dante sought to establish his dream of the restoration of the natural and universal *forma locutionis* of Eden. Yet unlike those in the Renaissance who wished to restore the Hebrew language itself to its original magic and divinatory power, Dante's goal was to reinstate these original conditions in a modern invention: an illustrious vernacular, of which his own poetry would constitute the most notable achievement, was, to Dante, the only way in which a modern poet might heal the wound of Babel. The entire second part of *De Vulgari Eloquentia* is therefore not to be understood as a mere treatise of style but as an effort to fix the conditions, rules, *forma locutionis* of the only conceivable perfect language: the Italian of the poetry of Dante. The illustrious vernacular would take from the perfect language its *necessity* (as opposed to conventionality) because, just as the perfect *forma locutionis* permitted Adam to speak with God, so Dante's language would permit the poet to make his words adequate to express what he wished and what could not be expressed otherwise.

Notice that from this bold conception for the restoration of a perfect language, and of his own role within it, comes a celebration of the quasi-biological force displayed by language's capacity to change and renew itself over time rather than a lament over the multiplicity of tongues. For someone of Dante's temperament, a conviction that the Hebrew of Adam was the one truly perfect language could only have resulted in his learning Hebrew and composing his poem in that idiom. That Dante did not decide to learn Hebrew shows that he was convinced that the vernacular he intended to invent would correspond to the principles of the universal, God-given form better even than the Hebrew spoken by Adam himself. Thus Dante puts forth his own candidacy as a new (and more perfect) Adam.

Once having improved his own personal perfect language, Dante could dare not only to descend into the infernal funnel and to climb up the mountain of Purgatory: he had the linguistical, poetical, and mystical force to fly to Paradise.

One could say that, since it was thinkable that in Paradise he could meet Adam, Dante went there (among many other reasons) to check with the hero of his little linguistic treatise the validity of his former assumptions.

Alas! Something strange happens. What Adam tells Dante about the language of Eden is exactly the contrary of what Dante conjectured in *De Vulgari Eloquentia!*

I repeat that Dante wrote *De Vulgari Eloquentia* between 1303 and 1305. The *Inferno* was made public in 1314, the *Purgatory* in

1315. It is possible that Dante started writing the *Paradise* at the same time, in Verona in about 1313, and as a matter of fact he sent the first Canto to Cangrande della Scala in 1316 with a letter (the famous Epistula XIII, which according to certain scholars was not written by Dante but nonetheless mirrors pretty well his ideas on the interpretation of his *Comedy*). Dante died in 1321, and, according to the legend, the last thirteen Cantos of the *Paradise* were found by his sons only after his death.

In any case between *De Vulgari Eloquentia* and the Canto XXVI there is a lapse of more than ten years, and in this period either Dante really met Adam in Paradise, learning from him something he did not previously know, or changed his mind for other reasons.

Please remember that in his earlier work Dante unambiguously stated that it was from the *forma locutionis*, given by God, that the perfect language of Hebrew was born and that it was in this perfect language that Adam addressed God, calling him *El*. In *Paradise* XXVI, 24–138, however, Adam says:

> La lingua ch'io parlai fu tutta spenta
> innanzi che all'ovra incomsummabile
> fosse la gente di Nembròt attenta:
> ché nullo effetto mai razionabile,
> per lo piacer uman che rinovella
> seguendo il cielo, sempre fu durabile.
> Opera naturale è ch'uom favella,
> ma, così o così, natura lascia,
> poi fare a voi, secondo che v'abbella.
> Pria ch'i' scendessi all'infernale ambascia
> *I* s'appellava in terra il sommo bene,
> onde vien la letizia che mi fascia;
> e *EL* si chiamò poi: e ciò convene,
> ché l'uso dei mortali è come fronda
> in ramo, che sen va e altra vene.

A literal translation would be:

The language that I spoke was entirely extinguished before the uncompletable work (the tower of Babel) of the people of Nembrot was even conceived. For no product of the human reason, from the human taste for always having something new, following the influence of the stars, is ever stable. It is natural that man speaks, but, whether this way or that, nature lets you do yourselves, as it pleases you. Before I descended into the pains of Hell, on earth the Highest Good was called *I*, from whence comes the light of joy that enfolds me. The name then became *EL*, and this change was proper, because the customs of mortals are like leaves on a branch, one goes and another comes.

This means that the Hebrew spoken before the building of the tower, when God was named *El*, was not the same as the Hebrew spoken in the earthly paradise, when Adam called Him *I*.

We are facing here a double problem: (1) Why did Dante change his mind? (2) Why did Dante choose the name *I*?

Let me deal first with the second question. Most of the interpreters say that the reasons for this choice are obscure. A first and absolutely ridiculous interpretation goes: *I* is the Roman numeral signifying the number one, the number of perfect unity. Ridiculous, because in Canto XIX, 128 of *Paradise* the Roman numeral for "I" stands for the smallest quantity, as opposed to *M*, which stands for one thousand, that is, for a great quantity. It would be curious to characterize God in terms of minimum value.

A second interpretation represents an odd case of confusion of tongues or the naive belief that one's own tongue is the only existing and perfect one. Take Dorothy Sayers's translation of the *Divine Comedy*, in which the last thirteen Cantos of the *Paradise* were translated by Barbara Reynolds, who also supplied the corresponding footnotes. (By the way, Dorothy Sayers died leaving thirteen Cantos untranslated, just as Dante was supposed not to have written or finished the same number.) The English translation reads:

Ere I descend to the pains of Hell
Jah was the name men called the highest Good
Which swathes me in this joy. Thereafter El
his title was on earth;

The translation is not so whimsical, also because in English *I* would have been interpreted as a pronoun. A whimsical remark appears however in the footnote, where Reynolds suggests that Dante was thinking of Psalm 68, line 4, which says "Sing unto God, sing praises to his name: extol him that rideth upon the heavens by his name Jah, and rejoice before him." Reynolds did not consider that unfortunately Dante not only could not read Hebrew but also could not have had the King James version on his desk. He knew only the *Vulgata*, and the *Vulgata* (where this psalm is numbered 67 rather than 68) translates the Hebrew as "Cantate Deo psalmum, dicite nomen ejus, iter facite ei qui ascendit super occasum. Deus est nomen illi. Exultate in conspectu ejus." Thus the only name of God is *Deus* (Luther, too, translated *Yah* as *Herr*, the Lord). In the same vein, one must drop the hypothesis that Dante found the name *IH* in *Exodus* 3:15, because there, too, the Vulgata speaks of *Deus*.

Equally weak seems to be the explanation according to which Dante intended by *I* the personal pronoun *io* in a shortened form accepted by Florentine vernacular. It is true that he knew that God said "Ego sum qui sum," but the name of God in this case would not be *Ego* ("I") but rather *Ehiè* ("the One Who is").[3]

There is a somewhat better explanation: Isidore of Seville in book VII, 15, of his *Etymologies* lists the traditional names of God according to the Hebrew tradition, and along with El, Eloi, Eloe, Sabaoth, Elion, Eie, Adonai, Tetragrammaton, Saddai, he also mentions Ia, because these are the last letters of *alleluia*. But if Dante, who certainly found El in Isidore, decided to shift to another name, why did he write *I* instead of *Ia*? Notice that if he used *Ia* instead of *I* the number of syllables in the his verse would not have changed, and so the solution was poetically feasible.

I think we cannot answer all these questions without first solving the previous problem, namely, why Dante changed his mind about the perfection of the original Hebrew of Adam.

In order to answer we have to step back and see what happened in the cabalistic milieu before the birth of Dante as well as during his life.

By the time of the confusion of Babel the language of Adam was, as Dante puts it, "tutta spenta" (entirely extinguished). This view of the historical evolution of the original Adamic language was not Dante's invention. For example, I find in Moshe Idel's *Language, Torah, and Hermeneutics in Abraham Abulafia* a surprising quotation from an unpublished manuscript by an anonymous disciple of Abulafia, where it is said that:

> Anyone who believes in the creation of the world, if he believes that languages are conventional he must also believe that they are of two types: the first is Divine, i.e., agreement between God and Adam, and the second is natural, i.e., based on agreement between Adam and Eve and their children. The second is derived from the first, and the first was known only to Adam and was not passed on to any of his offspring except for Seth. . . . And so, the tradition reached Noah. And the confusion of tongues during the generation of the dispersion occurred only to the second type of language, i.e., to the natural language.[4]

The lost language of Adam, which escaped the confusion of tongues, was certainly the cabalistic combinatorial ability to produce or reproduce the perfect discourse of the Eternal Torah by rereading in a unheard-of way the text written in the language of the historical Torah. As such it was a *forma locutionis*, a universal set of mystical rules.

For Abulafia, the Torah had to be equated with the Active Intellect, and the scheme from which God created the world was the same as the gift that He gave to Adam: a linguistic matrix, not yet Hebrew but capable of generating all other languages. There were Averroist influences on Abulafia that led him to believe in a single Active Intellect common to the entire human species. There were demonstrable and undoubted Averroist sympathies in Dante, too, especially in his version of the Avicennist concept of the Active Intellect (equated with Divine Wisdom) that offers the forms to possible intellect. Nor were the Modistae and the others who supported the idea of universal grammar exempt from Averroist influence. Thus there existed a common philosophical ground that, even without positing direct links, would have inclined both Dante and Abulafia to regard the gift of language as the bestowal of a *forma locutionis*, defined as a generative linguistic matrix with affinities to the Active Intellect.

Abulafia made a distinction between the twenty-two letters as a linguistic matrix and Hebrew as the mother tongue of mankind. The twenty-two Hebrew letters represented the ideal sounds that had presided over the creation of the seventy existing languages. The fact that other languages had more vowels depended on variations in pronouncing the twenty-two letters. The twenty-two Hebrew letters represented the entire gamut of sounds naturally produced by the human vocal organs. It was the different ways of combining these letters that had given rise to the different languages, some of them with more vowels. Abulafia admitted that the representation of these sounds according to certain graphic signs was a matter of convention; it was, however, a convention established between God and the prophets. Being aware that there existed other theories claiming that the sounds that expressed ideas of things were conventional (he could have encountered such an Aristotelian and Stoic notion in Jewish authors such as Maimonides), Abulafia, nevertheless, invoked a rather modern distinction between conventionality and arbitrariness, asserting that Hebrew was a conventional but not an arbitrary language. He rejected the claim, sustained by, among others, certain Christian authors, that, left entirely to itself, a child would automatically begin to speak Hebrew: the child would be unaware of the convention. Yet Hebrew remained the sacred mother tongue because the names given by Adam, though conventional, were *in accordance with nature*. In this sense, Hebrew was the protolanguage. Its existence was a precondition for all the rest, "for if such a language did not precede it, there could not have been mutual agreement to call a given object by a different name from what it was previously called, for how would the second person understand the second name if he does not know the original name, in order to be able to agree to the changes."[5]

Abulafia lamented that in the course of their exile his people had forgotten their original language. He looked on the cabalist as a laborer working to rediscover the original matrix of all the seventy languages of the world. Still, he knew that it would not be until the coming of the Messiah that all the secrets of the cabala would be definitively revealed. Only then, at the end of time, would all linguistic differences cease, and languages be reabsorbed back into the original Sacred Tongue.

This is not the only surprise provided by Abulafia, however. The *Cabala of the Names*, or the ecstatic cabala, was based in the practice of reciting the divine names hidden in the Torah by combining the letters of the Hebrew alphabet. In a process of free linguistic creativity, it altered, disarticulated, decomposed, and recomposed the textual surface to reach the single letters that served as its linguistic raw material.

And begin by combining this name, namely, YHWH, at the beginning alone, and examining all its combinations and move it, turn it about like a wheel, returning around, front and back, like a scroll, and do not let it rest, but when you see its matter strengthened because of the great motion, because of the fear of confusion of your imagination, and rolling about of your thoughts, and when you let it rest, return to it and ask [it] until there shall come to your hand a word of wisdom from it, do not abandon it. Afterwards go on to the second one from it,

Adonay, and ask of it its foundation [*yesodo*] and it will reveal to you its secret [*sodo*]. And then you will apprehend its matter in the truth of its language. Then join and combine the two of them [YHWH and *Adonay*] and study them and ask them, and they will reveal to you the secrets of wisdom. . . .

Afterwards combine Elohim, and it will also grant you wisdom, and then combine the four of them, and find the miracles of the Perfect One [i.e., God], which are miracles of wisdom.[6]

What justified this process of textual dissolution was that, for Abulafia, each letter, each atomic element, already had a meaning of its own, independent of the meaning of the syntagms in which it occurred. Each letter was already a divine name: "Since, in the letters of the Name, each letter is already a name itself, know that Yod is a name, and YH is a name" (*Perush Havdalah de-Rabbi 'Akiva*).[7]

Paleographers say that in certain codes of the *Divine Comedy I* is written as *Y*. Why can this not lead us to suppose that the *I* of Dante was the *YOD* of Abulafia, a divine name?

I have spoken of the idea of the evolution of the primeval Adamic Hebrew, of a possible doctrine of a common Active Intellect and of Yod as a name of God. None of these elements, taken separately, constitutes a proof. Taken together, they sound, to say the least, very intriguing. Could Dante have known the theories of Abulafia?

Abulafia visited Italy on several occasions: he was in Rome in 1260 (five years before the birth of Dante); he remained on the peninsula until 1271, when he returned to Barcelona; he returned to Rome in 1280 with the project of converting the pope. He journeyed afterward to Sicily, where all trace of him is lost somewhere near the end of the 1290s. His ideas incontestably exercised an influence on contemporary Italian Jewish thought.

We have a record of a debate in 1290 between Hillel of Verona (who had probably met Abulafia twenty years earlier) and Zerakhya of Barcelona, who arrived in Italy at the beginning of the 1270s.

Hillel, who had acquaintances in the world of Bolognese intellectuals, had written to Zerakhya to ask him the question first posed by Herodotus: in what language would a child speak if it were brought up with no linguistic stimuli? Hillel sustained that such a child would naturally speak Hebrew, because Hebrew was man's original natural language. Hillel either did not know or disregarded the fact that Abulafia was of a different opinion. Not so with Zerakhya. He sarcastically remarked that Hillel had been taken in by the siren song of the "uncircumcised" of Bologna. The first sounds emitted by a child without linguistic education, he asserted, would resemble the barking of dogs. It was madness to sustain that the sacred language could be naturally bestowed on man.

Man possessed a linguistic potential, but it was a potential that could be activated only through the education of the vocal organs. This, however, required instruction. At this point, Zerakhya brought forward a proof that recurs in a number of post-Renaissance Christian authors (for example, in Walton's *In Biblia polyglotta prolegomena* of 1673 or Vallesio's *De sacra philosophia* of 1652): had there been the primordial gift of an original sacred language, then all human beings, regardless of their native tongue, would have the innate ability to speak it.

The existence of this debate is enough to show, without the invention of a meeting between Dante and Abulafia, that Abulafia's ideas were subject to discussion in Italy, especially in the Bolognese intellectual circles that influenced Dante, and that from them, as Maria Corti argues, he absorbed his notion of the *forma locutionis*. Nor does the Bologna debate constitute the only point of encounter between Dante and Jewish thought.

I am using freely various bits of information on the Italian Jewish milieu in the Middle Ages provided by Jacqueline Genot-Bismuth (especially in her still-unpublished and huge research on Immanuel of Rome).[8] It is striking to notice how many things happened in the Jewish milieus in Verona, Forli, and Bologna, all places that Dante visited (and do not forget that Hillel was from Verona and that in Verona Dante wrote part of the *Paradise*). At the close of the thirteenth century, a scholar named Yehuda Romano gave a series of public readings of the *Divine Comedy* for his coreligionists; a Lionello de Ser Daniele did likewise using a *Divine Comedy* transliterated into Hebrew script; and the surprising personage Immanuel of Rome, in his own poetic compositions, seemed to launch an attack on Dante's ideals, almost aspiring to produce a sort of counter-Comedy in Hebrew.

Naturally such information only establishes the influence of Dante on Italian Jewish culture, not the other way around. Yet Genot-Bismuth is able to show opposing influences as well, even to the point of suggesting that Dante's theory of the four senses of scripture, found in his *Epistula* XIII, had a Jewish origin. Such a hypothesis may be too bold: there were any number of Christian sources from which Dante might have drawn this doctrine. What seems less daring and, in fact, entirely plausible is the suggestion that Dante would have heard echoes of the debate between Hillel and Zerakhya. One could say that in *De Vulgari Eloquentia* he appears still close to the position of Hillel (or that of the Christian inspirers for whom Zerakhya reproached Hillel), while in *Paradise* he turned toward the positions of Zerakhya, that is, the position of Abulafia.

Dante visited Forli in 1303, and in this same city Hillel presumably died about 1295. There is much discussion about whether Dante was in touch with Immanuel of Rome or not. I cannot thrust my nose into such specialized historical questions, and there are many legends surrounding the notion of such a connection, as there is still much debate as to the extent of the influence on Dante of Arab sources. The real problem is different. If, for instance, somebody asked whether my writings have been influenced by Dewey or Merleau-Ponty, the philological problem would not be whether I had actually met Dewey or Merleau-Ponty. The problem would be to establish, first, whether there are detectable literal or conceptual analogies between my work and theirs and, second, whether I had the physical possibility of reading the books of these thinkers (by the way, I never met either of them, but I have certainly read their books).

In other words, it is not necessary to document direct links but rather to demonstrate the existence of an intellectual climate in which ideas could circulate and in which formal and informal debate between the church and the synagogue might ensue. We should remember that, before the Renaissance, a Christian thinker would scarcely wish to admit publicly that he drew on Hebrew doctrine. Like heretics, the Jewish community belonged to a category of outcasts that—as Le Goff shrewdly observes—the Middle Ages officially despised but at the same time admired, regarding them with an admixture of attraction and fear, keeping them at a distance but making sure that the distance was fixed near enough so they would always remain close at hand. "What was termed charity in their regard more resembled the game that cats play with mice."[9]

Before it was rehabilitated by the humanist culture, Christianity knew little of the cabala. It was often simply regarded as a branch of the black arts. But Dante seems to have been informed about an excluded and underground culture in which, at least according to vulgar opinion, the cabala somehow belonged.

I am aware that my hypothesis is only a hypothesis, and I can at most encourage further exploration in that no-man's land that was, in the era of Dante, the borderline between two traditions that remained officially separated. I can only testify that, if one studies different theories about the Adamic language, one comes upon curious analogies that are either produced by a common Agent Intellect or by some historical contacts.

Perhaps, on his way to Paradise, Dante met, even if indirectly, Abulafia. I hope both men reached the same destination, where they are now talking to each other, making fun of our desperate efforts to ascertain if they had something in common. If by chance Adam has joined the party, only God knows what kind of language those three characters are speaking together. Perhaps the angels are providing an excellent service of simultaneous translation.

3 | FROM MARCO POLO TO LEIBNIZ

Stories of Intellectual Misunderstandings

The first essay of this book showed how misunderstandings can take place inside a given culture. They can also take place between different cultures, when people are unable to understand that these cultures have different languages and world visions. The fact that—through serendipity—those mistakes have led to new discoveries means only that even errors can produce interesting side effects.

When two different cultures meet, there is a shock, a result of their reciprocal diversity. At this point, there are three possibilities:

Conquest: The members of culture A cannot recognize the members of culture B as normal human beings (and vice versa) and define them as "barbarians," that is, etymologically stuttering and nonspeaking beings and therefore nonhuman or subhuman beings. There are only two further possibilities: to civilize them (that is, to transform people B into acceptable copies of people A) or to destroy them. This, for instance, is how European civilization subjugated African and Amerindian cultures.

Cultural pillage: The members of culture A recognize the members of culture B as the bearers of an unknown wisdom. Culture A may try to subjugate the members of culture B politically and militarily, but at the same time they respect their exotic culture and try to understand it and translate its elements into their own. Greek civilization succeeded in transforming Egypt into a Hellenistic kingdom, but Greek culture had admired Egyptian wisdom since the times of Pythagoras and tried to steal, so to speak, the secret of Egyptian mathematics, alchemy, magic, and religion. A similar curiosity about and admiration and respect for Egyptian wisdom reappeared in modern European culture, from the Renaissance down to our own day.

Exchange: This two-way process of reciprocal influence and respect is certainly reflected in the early contacts between Europe and China. At the time of Marco Polo and certainly at the time of Father Matteo Ricci, these two cultures were exchanging their secrets, the Chinese accepted from the Jesuit missionaries many aspects of European science, and the Jesuits brought to Europe many aspects of Chinese civilization (to such an extent that Italians and Chinese are still debating the question of who invented spaghetti).

Conquest, cultural pillage, and exchange are abstract models, and in reality there are a variety of cases in which these three attitudes are merged. There are also two other ways for cultures to interact. I am not interested in the first, *exoticism*, by which a given culture, through misinterpretation and aesthetic *bricolage*, invents an ideal image of a distant culture, such as the *chinoisieries* of the past, or Gauguin's Polynesia, or the Siddhartha syndrome of the hippies, or the Paris of Vincente Minelli.

The second phenomenon is more difficult to label, but let me essay for the moment a tentative definition. We (in the sense of human beings) travel and explore the world, carrying with us some "background books." These need not accompany us physically; the point is that we travel with preconceived notions of the world, derived from our cultural tradition. In a very curious sense we travel knowing in advance what we are on the verge of discovering, because past reading has told us what we are supposed to discover. In other words, the influence of these background books is such that, irrespective of what travelers discover and see, they will interpret and explain everything in terms of these books.

For example, all medieval tradition convinced Europeans of the existence of the unicorn, an animal that looked like a gentle and slender white horse with a horn on its muzzle. Because it was increasingly difficult to come upon unicorns in Europe (indeed, according to analytic philosophers, they do not exist, although I am not sure I agree), tradition decided that unicorns were living in exotic countries, such as the kingdom of Prester John in Ethiopia.

When Marco Polo traveled to China, he was obviously looking for unicorns. Marco Polo was a merchant, not an intellectual, and moreover, when he started traveling, he was too young to have read many books. But he certainly knew all the legends current in his time about exotic countries, so he was prepared to encounter unicorns, and he looked for them. On his way home, in Java, he saw some animals that resembled unicorns, because they had a single horn on their muzzles, and because an entire tradition had prepared him to see unicorns, he identified these animals as unicorns. But because he was naive and honest, he could not refrain from telling the truth. And the truth was that the unicorns he saw were very different from those represented by a millennial tradition. They were not white but black. They had pelts like buffalo, and their hooves were as big as elephants.' Their horns, too, were not white but black, their tongues were spiky, and their heads looked like wild boars.' In fact, what Marco Polo saw was the rhinoceros.

We cannot say Marco Polo lied. He told the simple truth, namely, that unicorns were not the gentle beasts people believed them to be. But he was unable to say he had found new and uncommon animals; instinctively, he tried to identify them with a well-known image. Cognitive science would say that he was determined by a cognitive model. He was unable to speak about the unknown but could only refer to what he already knew and expected to meet. He was a victim of his background books.

Let me consider now another story. As I discussed in the preceding chapter, for a long time European theologians, grammarians, and philosophers dreamed of rediscovering the language of the first man, Adam, lost since, according to the Bible, God confused the languages of mankind to punish the pride of those who wanted to build the Tower of Babel. The Adamic language had to be perfect because its names showed a direct analogy with the nature of things, and for a long time it was universally maintained that this perfect language corresponded to the original Hebrew.

Two hundred years after Marco Polo, at the beginning of the fifteenth century, European culture rediscovered Egyptian hieroglyphs. Their code was irremediably lost (rediscovered only in the nineteenth century by Champollion), but at that time a Greek manuscript, the *Hieroglyphica* of Horapollus (or Horus Apollon), that purported to decipher that code, was introduced into Italy, in Florence.

Today we know that sometimes hieroglyphs stand for the things of which they are the images, but more frequently they possess a phonetic value. Following the fabulous interpretation of Horapollus, however, the scholars of the fifteenth, sixteenth, and seventeenth centuries believed that they signified mysterious and mystical truths, understandable only by initiates. They were divine symbols, able to communicate not merely the names or forms of things but their very essences, their true and deeply mysterious meanings. They were thus considered the first instance of perfect language.

Horapollus's booklet seems to be a Greek translation of more ancient Egyptian texts. It is divided into short chapters that explain, for example, that the Egyptians represented age by depicting the sun and the moon or the month by a palm branch. In each case, there follows a brief description of the symbolic meaning of the figure and in many cases its polysemic value: for example, the vulture is said to signify mother, sight, the end of a thing, knowledge of the future, year, sky, mercy, Minerva, Juno, or two drachmas. Sometimes the hieroglyphic sign is a number: pleasure, for example, is denoted by the number 16, because (allegedly) sexual activity begins at the age of sixteen. Because it takes two to have intercourse, however, intercourse is denoted by a double 16.

We now know that Horapollus's text was a Hellenistic compilation dating from as late as the fifth century A.D., and although certain passages indicate that the author did possess exact information about Egyptian hieroglyphs, the *Hieroglyphica* seem to be based on some texts written a few centuries earlier. Horapollus was describing a written system whose last example is on the Theodosius temple (394 A.D.). Even if these inscriptions were still similar to those elaborated three thousand years before, the Egyptian language in the fifth century had radically changed. Thus, when Horapollus wrote his text, the key to understanding hieroglyphs had long been lost.

Hieroglyphic writing is undoubtedly composed, in part, of iconic signs. Some are easily recognizable, such as eagle, owl, bull, snake, eye, foot, man seated with cup in hand. Others are stylized: the hoisted sail, the almondlike shape for a mouth, the serrated line for water. Other signs, at least to the untrained eye, seem to bear only the remotest resemblance to the things they are supposed to represent; for instance, a little square stands for a seat, a semicircle represents bread. All these signs are *ideograms* that work by rhetorical substitution: thus an inflated sail serves to represent the wind; a man seated with a cup means drink; a cow's ear means to understand.

Because not everything can be represented ideographically, ancient Egyptians turned their ideograms into simple phonograms. Thus to represent a certain sound they put the image of a thing whose name sounded similar. To take an example from Champollion's first decipherment *a*, the mouth—in Egyptian, *ro*—was chosen to represent the Greek consonant *ro*. The eagle represented *a*, the jagged line for water represented *n*, and so on.[1]

The necessary premise for decipherment of hieroglyphs was supplied by a stroke of pure fortune, when one of Napoleon's soldiers discovered a trilingual text, the famous Rosetta stone, which bore an inscription in hieroglyphic, in demotic (a cursive, administrative script elaborated about 1000 B.C.), and in Greek. But the Rosetta stone was unknown both at the time of Horapollus and when his book was read by the Western World.

Horapollus, however, was not totally wrong in attributing mystic significance to the images. By the early Christian ages Egypt had already abandoned many of its ancient traditions, but knowledge of sacred writing was still preserved by priests living within the sacred enclosures of the ancient temples. Because the sacred writing no longer served any practical purpose but was used only for initiatory purposes, these last priests began to introduce complexities into it, playing with the ambiguities inherent in a form of writing that could be read either phonetically or ideographically. The discovery that by combining different hieroglyphs evocative visual emblems might be created inspired these last scribes to experiment with increasingly complicated and abstruse combinations, and they began to formulate a sort of cabalistic game, based, however, on images rather than letters. Thus was formed a halo of visual connotations and secondary meanings around the terms represented by phonetic signs, a *basso ostinato* of associated meanings that served to amplify the original semantic range of the terms. Horapollus, unable to read the hieroglyphs, received only imprecise information about their symbolical interpretation and transmitted it to the West. The West, in its turn, regarded the hieroglyphs as the work of the great Hermes Trismegistus himself and therefore as a source of inexhaustible wisdom.

While this mistake was fully comprehensible, the truth was not that simple.

The second part of *Hieroglyphica* is probably the work of the Greek translator Philippos, and it is there that appear a number of clear references to the late Hellenistic tradition of the *Physiologus* and other bestiaries, herbariums, and lapidaries that derive from it. Consider, for example, the case of the stork. When the *Hieroglyphica* reaches the stork, it says:

> How [do you represent] one who loves the father?
> If they wish to denote he who loves the father, they depict a stork. In fact, this animal, nourished by its parents, never separates itself from them but remains with them until their old age, repaying them with piety and deference.

The *Hieroglyphica* was certainly one of the sources of the *Emblemata* of Andrea Alciati in 1531. Thus it is not surprising to find

there a reference to the stork, which, as the text explains, nour-
ishes its offspring by bringing them pleasing gifts while bearing on
its back the worn-out bodies of its parents, offering them food
from its own mouth. The image that accompanies this description
in the 1531 edition shows a bird that flies bearing another on its
back. In subsequent editions, such as the one of 1621, this is replaced by the image of a bird flying with a worm in its beak for
its offspring waiting, mouths agape, in the nest.

Alciati's commentary refers to the passage in the *Hieroglyphica*
that describes the stork. Yet that text includes no reference to the
feeding of the young or the transport of the parents. These features
are mentioned, however, in a text from the fourth century A.D., the
Hexaemeron of Basil (VIII, 5). In other words, the information contained in the *Hieroglyphica* was already at the disposal of European
culture.

A search for pre-Renaissance traces of the stork is rewarded with
pleasant surprises. The *Cambridge Bestiary* (twelfth century) notes
that storks nourish their young with exemplary affection, "incu-
bat[ing] their nests so tirelessly that they lose their own feathers.
What is more, when they have moulted in this way, they in turn are
looked after by the babies, for a time corresponding in length to the
time which they themselves have spent in bringing up and cher-
ishing their offspring."[2] The accompanying image shows a stork
carrying in its beak a frog, obviously a dainty morsel for its young.

The *Cambridge Bestiary* took this idea from Isidore of Seville,
who, in the *Etymologiarum* (XII, vii), tells more or less the same
story. Who then are Isidore's sources? Saint Basil we have already
seen; other influences were Saint Ambrose (*Hexaemeron* V, 16, 53)
and possibly Celsus (cited in Origen, *Contra Celsum* IV, 98), and
Porphyry (*De abstinentia* III, 23, 1). These, in their turn, used Pliny's
Naturalis Historia (X, 32) as their source.

Pliny, of course, could have been drawing on an Egyptian tradition, if Aelian, in the second or third century A.D., could claim
(though without citing Pliny by name) that "storks are venerated
among the Egyptians because they nourish and honor their par-

ents when they grow old" (*De animalium natura* X, 16). But the idea can be traced back even further, to Plutarch (*De solertia animalium* 4), Cicero (*De finibus bonorum et malorum* II, 110), Aristotle (*Historia animalium*, IX, 7, 612b, 35), Plato (*Alcibiades* 135 E), Aristophanes (*The Birds* 1355), and finally Sophocles (*Electra* 1058). There is nothing to prevent us from imagining that Sophocles himself was drawing on ancient Egyptian tradition, but, even if he were, it is evident that the story of the stork has been part of occidental culture for as long as we might care to investigate.

It follows, then, that Horapollus did not reveal anything hot. To any reader familiar with medieval and classical culture, his booklet differs little from the bestiaries current in the preceding centuries. It merely adds some information about specifically Egyptian animals, such as the ibis and the scarab, and neglects to make some of the standard moralizing comments or biblical references. This was clear even to the Renaissance. In his *Hieroglyphica sive de sacris Aegyptorum aliarumque gentium literis* of 1556, Pierio Valeriano never tired of employing his vast stock of knowledge of classical and Christian sources to note the occasions where the assertions of Horapollus might be confirmed. Yet instead of reading Horapollus in the light of a previous tradition, he reexamines this whole tradition in the light of Horapollus.

I am speaking of the rereading of a text (or of a network of texts) that had not been changed during the centuries, a semiotic incident that, as paradoxical as some of its effects may have been, was, in terms of it own dynamic, quite easy to explain. Horapollus's text (*qua* text) differs little from other similar writings, which were previously known, yet the humanists read it as a series of unprecedented statements. The reason is simply that fifteenth-century readers saw it as coming from a *different* author. The text had not changed, but the voice supposed to utter it was endowed with a different charisma. This changed the way in which the text was received and the way in which it was consequently interpreted.

I have mentioned old background books that led people to see the unknown in the light of the already known. This is an example of the opposite phenomenon: a case in which something already known is reconsidered in a new and uncanny way in the light of an as-yet-unknown book. Thus, old and familiar as these images were, the moment they appeared as if transmitted not by the familiar Christian and pagan sources but by the ancient Egyptian divinities themselves, they took on a fresh and radically different meaning. The missing scriptural commentaries were replaced by allusions to vague religious mysteries. The success of the book was due to its vagueness. Hieroglyphs were regarded as initiatory symbols.

This is the way ancient Egyptian hieroglyphs were considered by one of the most learned man of the seventeenth century, the Jesuit Athanasius Kircher, mainly in his monumental *Oedypus Aegyptiacus* (1652–54). Kircher firmly believed that ancient Egyptian was the perfect, Adamic language, and, according to the "hermetic" tradition, he identified the Egyptian Hermes Trismegistus with Moses and said that hieroglyphs were Symbols, that is, expressions that referred to an occult, unknown, and ambivalent content. Kircher defined a symbol as "a *nota significativa* of mysteries, that is to say, that it is the nature of a symbol to lead our minds, by means of certain similarities, to the understanding of things vastly different from the things that are offered to our external senses, and whose property it is to appear hidden under the veil of an obscure expression. . . . Symbols cannot be translated by words, but expressed only be marks, characters, and figures."[3] The symbols were initiatory because they were wrapped in an impenetrable and indecipherable enigma, to protect them from the idle curiosity of the vulgar multitudes.

When Kircher set out to decipher hieroglyphs in the seventeenth century, there was no Rosetta stone to guide him. This explains his double mistake, namely, believing that hieroglyphs had only symbolic meaning and the absolutely fanciful way in which he identified their meaning. He did not base his work on Horapollus's fantastic bestiary; instead, he studied and made copies of the real hieroglyphic inscriptions, and his reconstructions, reproduced in sumptuous tables, have an artistic fascination all their own. Kircher poured elements of his own fantasy into these re-constructions, frequently reportraying the stylized hieroglyphs in curvaceous baroque forms.

At times, Kircher seemed close to the intuition that certain hi-eroglyphs had a phonetic value. He even constructed a rather imaginative alphabet of twenty-one hieroglyphs from whose forms he derived, through progressive abstractions, the letters of the Greek alphabet. But it was his conviction that, finally, hiero-glyphs all *showed* something about the natural world that prevent-ed him from ever finding the right track.

Thus in his *Obeliscus Pamphilius* Kircher reproduced the images of a cartouche to which he gave the following reading: "The orig-inator of all fecundity and vegetation is Osiris, whose generative power bears from heaven to his kingdom the Sacred Mophtha." This same image was deciphered by Champollion (who in his *Let-tre à Dacier* used Kircher's own reproduction) as AOTKPTA (auto-crat or emperor), son of the sun and sovereign of the crown, KHZPZ TMHTENZ ZBZTZ (Caesar Domitian Augustus)."[4] The difference is, to say the least, notable, especially as regards the mysterious Mophtha, seen as a lion, on which Kircher expended pages and pages of mystic exegesis listing its numerous properties, while for Champollion the lion stands for the Greek letter *lambda*.

Similarly, in the third volume of the *Oedypus* there is long analy-sis of a cartouche that appears on the Lateran obelisk, where Kircher read a long argument concerning the necessity of attracting the benefits of the divine Osiris and the Nile by means of sacred cere-monies activating the Chain of Genies, tied to the signs of the zo-diac. Egyptologists today read it as simply the name of the pharaoh Apries.

Kircher was then wildly wrong. Still, notwithstanding his even-tual failure, he is the father of Egyptology, though in the same way that Ptolemy is the father of astronomy: in spite of the fact that his main hypothesis was mistaken. By following a false hypothesis he collected real archeological material, and Champollion (more than one hundred fifty years later), lacking an opportunity for direct observation, used Kircher's reconstructions for his study of the obelisk standing in Rome's Piazza Navona.

Since we began by speaking of China, let us see what Kircher, insatiable in his lunatic curiosity, did with China. Egyptian was an original language, certainly more perfect than Hebrew and certainly more ancient, too. Why not look for other, more venerable linguistic ancestors?

Toward the end of the sixteenth century the Western world began to learn more about China, now visited not only by merchants and explorers, as in the days of Marco Polo. In 1569 the Dominican Gaspar da Cruz published a first description of Chinese writing (in his *Tractado en quem se contan muito por extenso as cousas de la China*), revealing that the ideograms did not represent sounds but things, or ideas of those things, to such an extent that they were understood by different peoples, including the Chinese, the Cochincinese, and the Japanese, even though these various peoples pronounced them in different ways. These revelations reappeared in a book by Juan Gonzalez de Mendoza (*Historia del gran reyno de la China*, 1585), who repeated that even though different oriental peoples were speaking different languages they could understand one another by writing ideograms that represented the same ideas for all of them. When in 1615 the diaries of Father Matteo Ricci were published, those ideas became a matter of common knowledge, and one of the authors of the most important project for a universal philosophical language, John Wilkins, wrote in his *Mercury* (1641) that "though [peoples] of China and Japan doe as much differ in their language, as the Hebrew and the Dutch, yet either of them can, by this help of a common character as well understood the books and letters of the others, as if they were only their own."[5]

The first European scholar to speak of a "universal character" was Francis Bacon (*De dignitate et augmentis scientiarum*, 1623, vi, 1), and, in order to prove its possibility, he cited Chinese writing. Curiously enough, neither Bacon nor Wilkins understood the iconic origin of ideograms, and both took them as purely conventional devices. In any case, the ideograms seemed to be endowed with the double property of being universal and also capable of establishing a direct contact between the character and the idea. The discovery of Chinese ideograms had an enormous influence on the development of the search for a universal philosophical language in Europe.

Fascinated as they were by reports of China, some thinkers discovered that Chinese imperial genealogies went further back in time than biblical ones. Thus Isaac de la Peyrère in 1655 (*Systema Theologicum ex prae-Adamitarum hypothesis*) ventured the provocative hypothesis of a mankind prior to Adam. The whole of Hebrew and Christian sacred history (comprehending original sin and the mission of Jesus Christ) thus concerned only the Hebrew people but not the peoples of more ancient lands such as China. Needless to say, this hypothesis was considered heretical and did not enjoy great success, but it is worth recalling because it shows to what an extent China was increasingly seen as the land of an unknown wisdom.

The problem was to bring China into the framework of familiar wisdom. Thus in 1699 we see John Webb (in his *Historical essay endeavouring the probability that the language of the empire of China is the primitive language*) making a different hypothesis: after the Flood, Noah and his Ark did not land on top of Mount Ararat in Armenia but instead in China. Thus the Chinese language is the purest version of Adamic Hebrew, and only the Chinese, having lived for millennia without suffering foreign invasions, preserved it in its original purity.

Peyrère was a Protestant, Webb an Anglican. Dealing with the fascination of the Chinese enigma, the Catholic Church reacted in a different way. As early as 1540 Jesuit missionaries had sailed toward the Portuguese domain in Asia. Saint Francis Xavier tried to evangelize China. In 1583 Matteo Ricci arrived at Macao and at the beginning of the seventeenth century began a new approach to Chinese culture, deciding to become "a Chinese among Chinese."

But let us return to Kircher. He was fascinated by Chinese civilization and for years collected all the information brought back to Europe by his fellow Jesuits. This led to his publication in 1667 of an enormous, beautiful book on Chinese marvels and secrets: *China Illustrata* (*China illustrated through its monuments, both sacred and prophane etc . . .*).

This book represented a sort of encyclopedia of China, covering landscape, customs, dress, daily life, religion, animals, flowers, plants and minerals, architecture and mechanical arts, and language, starting from the analysis of a Nestorian inscription found in China in 1625, which, according to Kircher, proved an early penetration of Christianity into this country.

The information Kircher collected was probably precise. While in the 1561 edition of Ptolemy's *Geography* China was still fabulously and imprecisely represented, in Kircher's book the map of the country is extraordinarily accurate and detailed, at least by the cartographic standards of that time. But if the information was precise, Kircher's interpretation of it was dominated by the baroque taste for wonders. Some of the pictures in the book are artistically curious and fascinating and demonstrate that Kircher, giving instruction to the artists on the basis of information received, acted as Marco Polo and other precious travelers had, interpreting verbal reports according to his own background books. Among them were certainly many nonscientific and fabulous descriptions of exotic countries, and there is a trace of this influence in the illustrations. Some unheard-of animals and plants evoke things that Kircher's informants had actually met, even though, in reporting them, they added fantastic details; others, such as a dragon fighting a leopard (allegedly an account from the province of Kiamsi), showed that Kircher or his informant did not distinguish clearly between direct experience and local legends.

Since he was convinced that the Chinese were influenced very early by Christian ideas, Kircher did his best to describe the Chinese gods as reflecting Christian mysteries like the Holy Trinity. And, further, influenced as he was by one of his own previous books, *Oedypus Aegyptiacus*, he wanted to demonstrate that Chinese culture originated with Egypt, and he interpreted any piece of information as evidence supporting his thesis.

Kircher starts with his adamant belief that every aspect of Chinese wisdom was brought to the country by the third son of Noah, Ham, who became an Egyptian pharaoh, inventor of idolatry and magic (and hence to be identified with Zoroaster), whose adviser was Hermes Trismegistus himself. Ham led his people through Persia to Bactria and beyond the kingdom of Mogor, and from there the Egyptian knowledge passed to China. Thus Kircher interpreted Confucius as the Chinese version of Hermes Trismegistus, and when he was told about certain Buddhist sculptures, he concocted from their description the image of curious divinities, one of which he unhesitantly identified with the Egyptian Isis. And though he understood from his informers' sketches what real pagodas were like, he was particularly struck by the description of a zigguratlike tower in the province of Fukien and immediately found an analogy with pyramids.

According to this line of thought Kircher carefully studied Chinese ideograms (following precise information from his informers) and understood what his predecessors, such as Bacon, had not, namely, that they must originally have portrayed the shapes of the things they represented. His method of tracing ideograms back to figures of ants or fish is rather whimsical, but his main purpose was to show that they derived from Egyptian hieroglyphs. According to his theory (as he wrote in both *Oedypus* and *China*), Ham obviously brought Egyptian writing to China, and consequently there was a close connection between hieroglyphics and ideograms.

Naturally, Kircher understood, as Bacon and others had, that ideograms were universal characters referring to ideas and not, alphabetically, to sounds. But at this point he took a curious position. While the hieroglyphs were of divine origin because they depicted the unknown and mysterious essence of things, Chinese ideograms referred clearly and unambiguously to precise ideas. In this sense they were corrupted hieroglyphs, which had lost their divine power and become mere practical tools. As Kircher said, when a hieroglyphic represents an animal that, in its turn, represents the sun, this sun is not only the celestial body but also the Sun as a spiritual archetype. Because the Chinese ideogram referred only to the sun as a star, it was a degenerate hieroglyph.

In the following century, in an atmosphere of neopagan sinophilia, the rationalistic criticism of Rousseau, Warburton, and the *Encyclopédie* of Diderot and D'Alembert turned the entire matter upside down: Chinese ideograms were better than Egyptian hieroglyphics because they were clear, precise, and unambiguous, while the hieroglyphs were vague and imprecise. But for Kircher such vagueness, the multiinterpretablity of hieroglyphics, was a proof of their divine origin, while the human precision of the ideogram was proof that true Egyptian wisdom (of which Christian wisdom was considered the direct heir) in coming to China was corrupted by the devil.

In order better to clarify Kircher's position, I must tell another story, one concerning the first description of the newly discovered lands of America, in particular the Mexican Maya and Aztec civilizations.

In 1590 a *Historia natural y moral de las Indias* was published by Father José de Acosta, who sought to demonstrate that the native inhabitants of America had a cultural tradition and outstanding intellectual abilities. To prove this, he described the pictographic nature of Mexican writing, showing that it had the same nature as Chinese. This was a courageous position because other authors had insisted on the subhuman nature of the Amerindians, and a work by Diego de Landa entitled *Relacion de las cosas de Yucatan* showed the diabolical nature of their writing.

Now it happens that Kircher (in *Oedypus*) shared the opinion of Diego de Landa and provided proof of the inferiority of Mexican writing. Their system was not made up of hieroglyphs, because, contrary to Egyptian hieroglyphs, the Mexican signs did not refer to sacred mysteries; neither were they ideograms in the Chinese sense, because they did not refer to general ideas but to singular facts. Instead, they were mere pictograms and thus not an example of universal language, because images referring—as mnemonic devices—to single facts can be understood only by those who already know these facts.

Recent research has proved that the Amerindians' pictograms were in fact an instance of a very flexible pictoral language, also able to express abstract ideas. It really is a pity that Western scholars finally discovered this only some centuries after we had destroyed those civilizations on the grounds of their semiotical inferiority.

But this is not only a case of new discoveries being influenced by backround books; it is a disquieting instance of the influence of political and economic motivations on the reading of newly discovered books.

Ancient Egypt had disappeared, and its whole wisdom had become part of the Christian civilization (at least, according to the Kircherian utopia); its writing was thus considered sacred and magical. Amerindians were people to be colonized; their religion had to be destroyed along with their political system (and as a matter of fact at the time Kircher was writing, both had already been destroyed). To justify such a violent transformation of a country and a culture, it was useful to demonstrate that their writing had no philosophical interest.

China, on the contrary, was a powerful empire with a developed culture; at that time, at least, the European states had no intention to subjugate it. *China Illustrata*, however, appeared under the auspices of Emperor Leopold I, whose dominions faced eastward and to whom Christian communities of the Asiatic Near East looked for protection (for instance, to please the Armenians it was suggested that the Holy Roman Emperor had a mission to rebuild the fabled but decaying temple of King Cyrus). Many of the Jesuit missionaries, such as Grueber and Martini, came from Central Europe, and Austria considered itself the great light of Eastern Christianity. In some way, the great empire of China had to be involved in such an ambitious project. Thus Kircher—who played a crucial part in the quest for this utopia—constructed a whole spiritual history of

China in which Christianity is claimed to have been an abiding force there since the early centuries after Christ. Even the connection he posited between China and Egypt was part of the imperial dream. China was presented not as an unknown barbarian to be defeated but as a prodigal son who should return to the home of the common Father.

Thus the problem was to deal with Chinese, to establish not a conquest but at least an exchange relationship, an exchange, however, in which Europe would play a major role, since it was the bearer of the true religion. The Mexicans, with their diabolical way of writing, had to be converted against their will; the Chinese, whose writing was neither as venerable as Egyptian nor as diabolical as Mexican, had to be peacefully and rationally persuaded of the superiority of Western thought. The Kircherian classification of hieroglyphics, ideograms, and pictograms mirrored the difference between two ways of interacting with exotic civilizations.

I have repeated the whole story because it seems to me that, once again, Kircher was ideally going to China not to discover something different but to find again and again what he already knew and what had been told him by a series of background books. Instead of trying to understand differences Kircher looked for identities.

Naturally, everything depends on one's background books and on what one is looking for. Let me finish with another story. At the end of the seventeenth century Leibniz was still looking for a universal language. But he was no longer pursuing the utopia of a perfect mystical tongue. Instead, he was searching for a mathematical language by virtue of which scholars, when debating a problem, could sit around a table, make some logical calculuses, and find a common truth. In short, he was a forerunner, or rather the founder, of contemporary formal logic.

His background books were different from those of Kircher, but his way of interpreting an unfamiliar culture was not so different. Profoundly fascinated by China (he devoted many writings to it), he thought that "by singular will of destiny" the two greatest civilizations of humanity were located at the two extremities of the Eurasian continent: Europe and China. He said that China was challenging Europe in the fight for primacy and that the battle was won now by one and now by the other of the two rivals. China was better than Europe as far as the elegance of life and the principles of ethics and politics were concerned, while Europe had achieved primacy in abstract mathematical sciences and metaphysics. Clearly, this was a man who did not harbor thoughts of political conquest or religious conversion but on the contrary was inspired by ideals of loyal and respectful mutual exchange of experiences.

After Leibniz had published a collection of documents on China (*Novissima Sinica*, 1679), Father Joachim Bouvet, just coming back from China, wrote him a letter in which he describes the *I Ching*, the now all-too-famous Chinese book on which many New Age fans are playing Olympic games of free and irresponsible interpretation. Father Bouvet thought that this book contained the fundamental principles of Chinese tradition. At the same time Leibniz was working on binary calculus, the mathematical calculus that proceeds by 0 and 1 and is still used today for programming computers. Leibniz was convinced that this calculus had a metaphysical foundation because it reflects the dialectic between God and Nothingness. Bouvet thought that binary calculus was perfectly represented by the structure of the hexagrams that appeared in the *I Ching*, and he sent Leibniz a reproduction of the system.

Now, in the *I Ching* the hexagrams follow the order (called Weng-Wang order) shown in figure 1, to be read horizontally from right to left. Bouvet, however, sent Leibniz a different representation (the Fu-hsi order), that is, the one reproduced in the central square of figure 2. It was easy for Leibniz, reading them horizontally (but from left to right!) to recognize in these representations a diagrammatic reproduction of the progression of natural numbers in binary digits, as he demonstrated in his *Explication de l'arithmétique binaire* (1705) (see figure 3). Thus—following Leibniz—we could say today that the *I Ching* contains the principles of Boolean algebra.

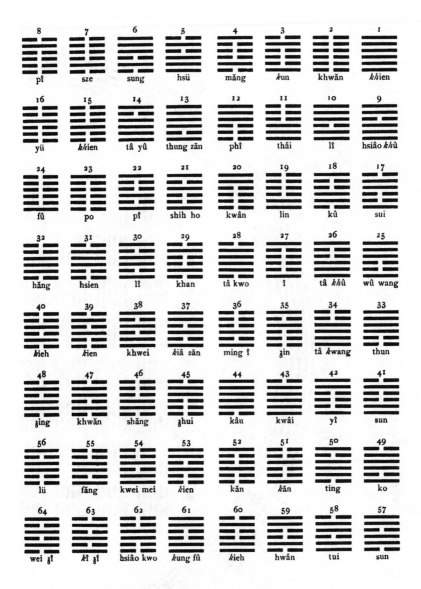

8	7	6	5	4	3	2	1
pî	sze	sung	hsü	măng	*k*un	khwăn	*kh*ien

16	15	14	13	12	11	10	9
yü	*kh*ien	tâ yü	thung zăn	phî	thâi	lî	hsiâo *kh*û

24	23	22	21	20	19	18	17
fû	po	pî	shih ho	kwăn	lin	kû	sui

32	31	30	29	28	27	26	25
hăng	hsien	lî	khan	tâ kwo	î	tâ *kh*û	wû wang

40	39	38	37	36	35	34	33
*k*ieh	*k*ien	khwei	*k*iâ zăn	ming î	₃in	tâ *k*wang	thun

48	47	46	45	44	43	42	41
₃ing	khwăn	shăng	₃hui	kâu	kwâi	yî	sun

56	55	54	53	52	51	50	49
lü	făng	kwei mei	*k*ien	kăn	*k*ăn	ting	ko

64	63	62	61	60	59	58	57
wei ₃î	*k*î ₃î	hsiâo kwo	*k*ung fû	*k*ieh	hwân	tui	sun

FIGURE I | The Hexagrams in the Weng-Wang Order

FIGURE 2 | The Hexagrams in the Fu-hsi Order

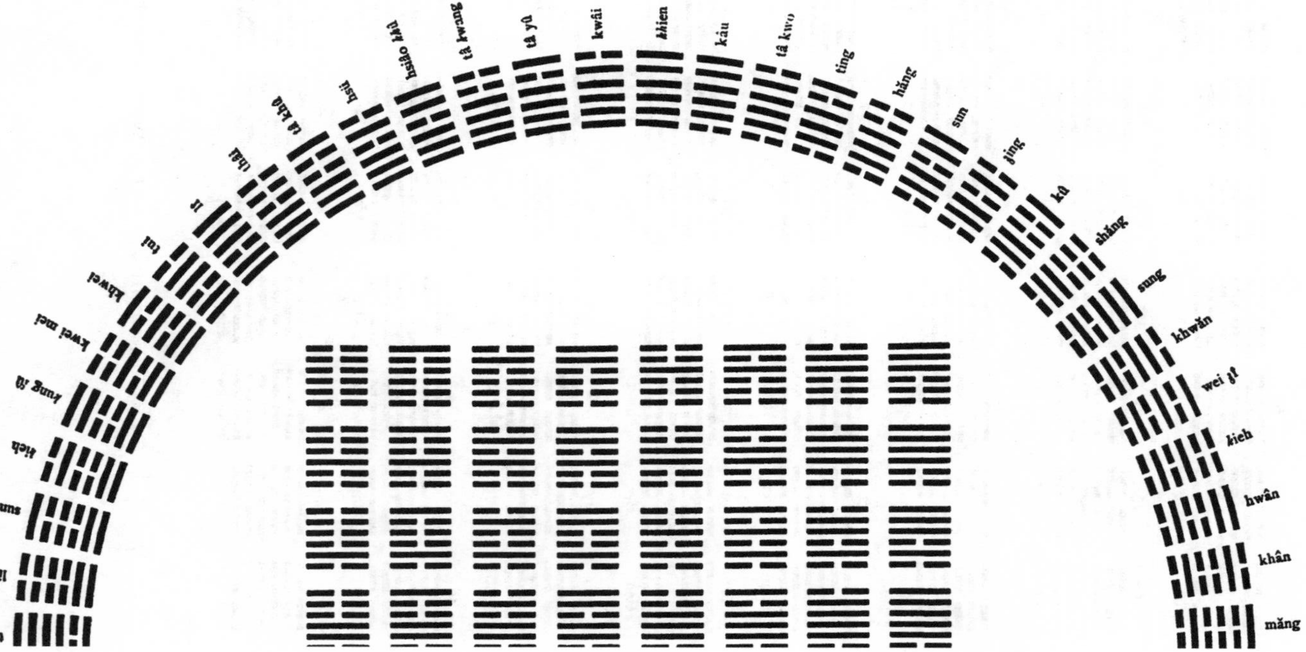

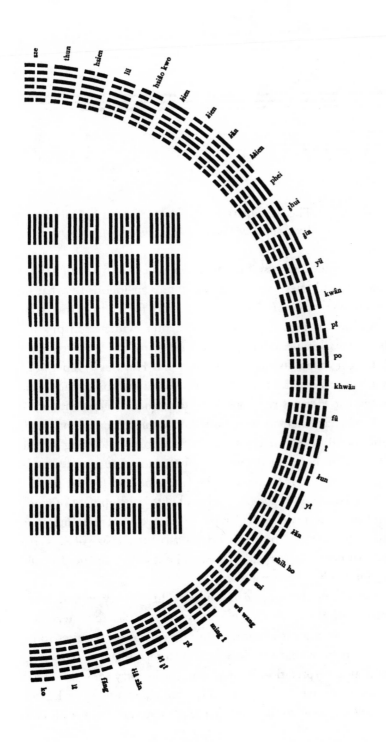

000	100	010	110	001	101	011	111
0	1	10	11	100	101	110	111
0	1	2	3	4	5	6	7

FIGURE 3 | The Presentation of Binary Calculus in Leibniz's
Explication de l'arithmétique binaire

This is another case in which someone discovers something different and tries to see it as absolutely analogous to what he already knows. The *I Ching* was important for its divinatory contents, but for Leibniz it becomes further evidence in proving the universal value of his formal calculus (and in a letter to Father Bouvet he suggests that its inventor was Hermes Trismegistus; as a matter of fact, Fu-hsi, the legendary inventor of the hexagrams, like Hermes was considered the father of all inventions).

Kircher and Leibniz were both illustrations of serendipity: both misunderstood Chinese writing, but the former, looking for the China of his hermetic dream, contributed to a future understanding of Chinese writing, while the latter, looking for the mathematical awareness of Fu-hsi, contributed to development of modern logic. But if we can be happy for every case of serendipity, we cannot forget that Columbus did miscalculate the size of the earth and that both Kircher and Leibniz did not follow the golden rule of sound cultural anthropology.

But what does sound cultural anthropology mean? I am not among those who believe there are no rules for interpretation, for even a programmatic misinterpretation requires some rules: I believe that there are at least intersubjective criteria to tell if an interpretation is a bad one, in the very sense in which we are sure that Kircher misinterpreted some aspects of Egyptian and Chinese culture and that Marco Polo did not really see unicorns. However, the real problem does not so much concern rules as our eternal drive to think that our rules are the golden ones.

The real problem of a critique of our own cultural models is to ask, when we see a unicorn, if by any chance it is not a rhinoceros.

4 | THE LANGUAGE OF THE AUSTRAL LAND

The subject of a perfect language has appeared in the cultural history of every people. Throughout the first period of this search,
which continued until the seventeenth century, this utopia consisted in the search for the primigenial Hebrew in which God
spoke to Adam or that Adam invented when giving names to the
animals and in which he had had his first dialogue with Eve. But
already in Dante's *De Vulgari Eloquentia* another possibility had
been broached: that God had not given Adam primordial Hebrew
but rather a general grammar, a transcendental form with which
to construct all possible languages.

But this possibility was situated on the two horns of a dilem-
ma. On the one hand, it was possible to conceive of a Chomskian
God, who gave Adam some deep syntactical structures common
to every language subsequently created by the human race, obey-
ing a universal structure of the mind (without waiting for Chomsky, Rivarol, an eighteenth-century author, had defined French as
the language of reason, because its direct order of discourse repro-
duces the logical order of reality). On the other hand, it could be
supposed that God had given Adam some semantic universals
(such as *high/low, to stand up, to think, thing, action,* and so on), a system of atomic notions by means of which every culture organizes
its own view of the world.

Until the arrival of Humboldt, even if one accepted the so-
called Epicurean hypothesis by which every people invents its
own language to deal with its own experience, no one dared pre-
figure anything similar to the Sapir-Whorf hypothesis: that it is

language that gives form to our experience of the world. Thinkers like Spinoza, Locke, Mersenne, and Leibniz admitted that our definitions (of *man*, *gold*, and so on) depend on our point of view about these things. Nobody, however, denied that it was possible to design a general system of ideas that somehow reflected the way the universe works.

Still, even before Dante, Ramon Lull had conceived the idea that there were universal notions, present in the language and in the thought of every people; he even believed that, by articulating and combining these concepts common to all men, it would be possible to convince the infidels—namely, the Moslems and the Jews—of the truth of the Christian religion.

This idea was revived at the dawn of the seventeenth century, after the discovery of Chinese ideograms, which were the same in Chinese, Japanese, and Korean (though pronounced differently), for these different peoples referred to the same concepts. The same thing, it was said, happens with numbers, where different words refer to the same mathematical entity. But numbers possessed another attractive aspect: independently of the variety of languages, all peoples (or very many of them) indicated them with the same cipher or character.

The idea that began to circulate, especially in Anglo-Saxon circles, inspired by the Baconian reform of knowledge, was this: postulate a priori a system of semantic universals, assign to each semantic atom a visual character or a sound, and you will have a universal language. As for the grammar, it would be a question, according to the project, of reducing the declensions or the conjugations themselves in order to derive the various elements of speech from a same root, indicating them with diacritical signs or some other criterion of economy.

The first idea of a universal character appeared in Francis Bacon and was to produce in England an abundant series of attempts, of which we would mention only those of George Dalgarno, Francis Lodwick, and John Wilkins. These inventors of languages, which will be called philosophic and a priori, because they were constructed on the basis of a given philosophical view of the world, no longer aimed merely at converting the infidel or recovering that mystic communion with God that distinguished the perfect language of Adam but rather at fostering commercial exchange, colonial expansion, and the diffusion of science. It is no accident that most of these attempts were linked to the work of the Royal Society in London, and many of the results—apparent failures—of these utopists contributed to the birth of the new scientific taxonomies.

But this project, even if abundantly stripped of the mystic-religious connotations of earlier centuries, had another feature in common with the yearned-for perfect language of Adam. It was said of Adam that he had given "proper" names to things, the names that the things should have as they expressed their nature. In earlier centuries and still in the heyday of the occult and the cabalistic speculations of the seventeenth century (consider, above all, Athanasius Kircher), this kinship between names and things was understood in terms of onomatopoeia, on the basis of far-fetched etymologies. To give an idea of the flavor of these ways of thinking, it suffices to quote Estienne Guichard (*L'harmonie étymologique des langues*, 1606), where, for example, the author shows how from the Hebrew word *batar* was derived the Latin synonym *dividere*. Shuffling the letters, the word becomes *tarab*, and from *tarab* derives the Latin *tribus*, which then leads to *distribuo* and finally to *dividere*.[1] *Zacen* means "old"; transposing the radicals one gets *zanec*, whence the Latin *senex*, and with a subsequent shift of letters comes *cazen*, whence in Oscan *casnar*, from which the Latin *canus* would be derived (247).

In subsequent attempts, the criterion of correspondence, or isomorphism between word and thing, is, by contrast, "compositional": the semantic atoms are named arbitrarily, but their combination is motivated by the nature of the designated object. This criterion is similar to that followed by chemistry today: calling hydrogen H, oxygen O, and sulphur S is surely arbitrary, but calling water H_2O or sulphuric acid H_2SO_4 is motivated by the chemical nature of these compounds. If either the order or the nature of the symbols were altered, another possible compound would be designated. Naturally this language is universal because, while each people indicates water with a different linguistic term, all are able to understand and write chemical symbols in the same way.

The search for a priori philosophic languages and the impassioned debates and rejections they inspired are evidenced by those pages in *Gulliver's Travels* where Swift imagines an assembly of professors bent on improving the language of their country. The first project, you will recall, was to abbreviate speech, reducing all polysyllables to monosyllables and eliminating verbs and participles. The second tended to abolish all words completely, because it was quite possible to communicate by displaying things (a difficult project because the so-called speakers would be obliged to carry with them a sack containing all the objects they planned to mention).

But even earlier the subject of the philosophic language had rightfully entered the literary genre of seventeenth-century utopias. For that matter, already in the Basel edition (1518) of More's *Utopia*, published by Pieter Gilles, there was an illustration with writing in the language of that ideal island; Godwin spoke of the possible language of the Selenites in his *Man in the Moone*; and Cyrano de Bergerac mentioned other planetary languages several times, both in *Les estats et les empires de la lune* and *Les estats et les empires du soleil*.

Still, if we want two models of language that echo the a priori philosophical language of the Utopians, we must turn to two novels narrating journeys in the Austral Land, *La Terre australe connue* (1676), by Gabriel de Foigny, and *L'Histoire des Sevarambes* (1677–79), by Denis Vairasse. Here, I will delve only into the first, which to me seems particularly instructive because, as often happens with good caricatures, the parodistic deformation reveals some essential features of the caricatured object.

La Terre australe connue is naturally a work of the imagination. In distant, unknown lands an ideal community is supposedly discovered. In this ideal community the language, too, is ideal, and it is interesting to remark that Foigny writes in 1676, after the three significant a priori philosophic language projects have appeared:

Lodwick's *Common Writing* (1647), Dalgarno's *Ars Signorum* (1661), and Wilkins's *Essay Towards a Real Character* (1668).

Foigny's exposition, precisely because it is incomplete and a burlesque, takes up only a few pages of his ninth chapter, rather than the five hundred (in folio!) of Wilkins's, the most voluminous and complete of all the projects of that century. Yet it is worth taking Foigny's into consideration because, for all its terseness, it illustrates the advantages and limitations of a philosophic language. It reveals and magnifies—as only a parody can—the flaws of its models, but, as they are magnified, the better we are able to distinguish them.

In order to better understand Foigny it is useful to see table 1 where I try to extrapolate from his text a sort of Austral dictionary, along with some grammatical rules. Because the author is often reticent, I have inferred some rules from examples, while others remain unspecific (thus, for example, of thirty-six accidentals, I have been able to reconstruct only eighteen).

Foigny's Austral inhabitants,

> to express their thoughts, employ three modes, all used in Europe: signs, voice, and writing. Signs are very familiar to them, and I have noticed that they spend many hours together without speaking in any other way, because they are ruled by this great principle: "that it is useless to employ several ways of action, when one can act with few."
> So they speak only when it is necessary to express a long series of propositions. All their words are monosyllabic, and their conjugations follow the same criterion. For example, *af* means "to love"; the present is *la, pa, ma*: I love, thou lovest, he loves; *lla, ppa, mma*: we love, you love, they love. They possess only one past tense, which we call the perfect: *lga, pga, mga*, I have loved, thou hast loved, etc.; *llga, ppga, mmga*, we have loved, etc. The future *lda, pda, mda*, I will love, etc., *llda, ppda, mmda*, we will love, etc. "To work," in the Austral language, is *uf: lu, pu, mu*, I work, thou workest, etc.; *lgu, pgu, mgu*, I have worked, etc.

SIMPLE BODIES
a – fire
e – air
i – water
o – salt
u – earth

QUALITIES
(ai – calm)
b – clear
c – hot
d – nasty
f – dry
g – bad
h – low
j – red
l – wet
m – desirable
n – black
p – sweet
q – pleasant
r – bitter
s – white
t – green
x – cold
z – high

ACTIONS
AF to love
UF to work

MORPHOLOGICAL
SIGNS
I – I
p – you
m – he/she/it (plural when doubled)
g – past
d – future

VERBAL FORMS
LA, PA, MA I love, Thou lovest, He loves
LLA, PPA, MMA We love, You love,
  They love
LGA, PGA, MGA I have loved, Thou hast
  loved, He has loved
LLGA, PPGA, MMGA We have loved,
  You have loved, They have loved

LDA, PDA, MDA I will love ... etc.
LLDA, PPDA, MMDA We will love ... etc.

EXAMPLES OF COMPOUND WORDS

AEB	*stars* (FIRE + AIR + CLEAR)
AAB	*sun* (FIRE + FIRE + CLEAR)
OEF	*birds* (SALT + AIR + DRY)
UEL	*man* (EARTH + AIR + WET)
AF	*to love* (FIRE + DRY)
LA	*I love (the secretion that love produces in us)*
PA	*thou lovest (lover's sweetness)*
EB	*clear air*
IC	*hot water*
IX	*cold water*
AF	*dry fire*
ES	*white air*
IPM	*sweet and desirable apple*
IRD	*nasty and unpleasant fruit*

TABLE I |

They have no declensions, no article, and very few words. They express simple things with a single vowel and compound things through vowels that indicate the chief simple bodies that make up those compounds. They know only five simple bodies, of which the first and most noble is fire, which they express with *a*; then there is air, indicated with *e*; the third is salt, indicated with *o*; the fourth, water, which they call *i*; and the fifth, earth, which they define as *u*.

As differentiating principle they employ the consonants, which are far more numerous than those of the Europeans. Each consonant denotes a quality peculiar to the things expressed by the vowels, thus *b* means clear: *c*, hot; *d*, unpleasant; *f*, dry, etc. Following these rules, they form words so well that, listening to them, you understand immediately the nature and the content of what they signify. They call the stars *Aeb*, a word that indicates their compound of fire and air, united to clarity. They call the sun *Aab*, birds are *Oef*, sign of their solidity and their aeriform and dry matter. Man is called *Uel*, which indicates his substance, partly aerial, partly terrestrial, accompanied by wetness. And so it is with other things. The advantage of this way of speaking is that you become philosophers, learning the prime elements, and in this country, nothing can be named without explaining at the same time its nature, which would seem miraculous to those unaware of the secret that they use to this end.

If their way of speech is so admirable, even more so is their writing . . . and though to us it seems very difficult to decipher them, custom makes the practice very simple.

Instructions in the manner of writing follow; here vowels are indicated with dots marked in different positions, while the thirty-six consonants of the alphabet are little strokes that surround the dots and are recognized by their angles. Foigny mentions these graphic devices, obviously making fun of similarly complicated systems, such as, for example, Joachim Becher's *Character pro notia linguarum universalis*, which proposes a form of notation capable of completely muddling the reader's ideas. He then continues, citing composites that can be achieved:

For example: *eb*, clear air; *ic*, hot water; *ix*, cold water; *ul*, damp earth; *af*, dry fire; *es*, white air. . . . There are another eighteen or nineteen, but in Europe we have no consonants corresponding to them.

The more you consider this way of writing, the more you will discover secrets worthy of admiration: *b* means clear; *c* hot; *x* cold; *l* wet; *f* dry; *n* black; *t* green; *d* nasty; *p* sweet; *q* pleasant; *r* bitter; *m* desirable; *g* bad: *z* high; *h* low; *j* red; *a* joined with *i*, calm. The moment a word is spoken, they know the nature of what it denotes: to indicate a sweet and desirable apple, they write *ipm*; nasty and unpleasant fruit is *ird*. I cannot explain all the other secrets that they understand and reveal in their letters.

The verbs are even more mysterious than the nouns. For example, they write and pronounce *af*, to say "to love"; *a* means fire, *f* means the scorching caused by love. They say *la* to mean "I love," which means the secretion that love produces in us; *pa*, "thou lovest," sign of the lover's sweetness; *lla*, "we love," the double *ll* indicating the number of persons; *oz* means "to speak," the letter *o* standing for salt, which seasons out speech, while *z* indicates the inhaling and exhaling necessary to speech.

When a child is being taught, the meaning of all the elements is explained to him, and when he unites them, he learns both the essence and the nature of all the things he is saying. This is a wonderful advantage both for the individual and for society, because, when they have learned to read, as they always do by the age of three, they understand at the same time all the characteristics of all beings.

In this language the single letters are chosen arbitrarily, and each refers to a simple notion or to a thing. When compound entities are denoted, however, the syntax of expression appears isomorphic with reference to the content. Assuming that stars are a compound of fire and clear-colored air, the syntagm *aeb* expresses "naturally" the nature of the thing. The expression is isomorphic to the content, to such a degree that changing one element of the expression denotes a different content. In fact, *aab* does not mean stars; it means *sun* because (in the astronomy of the Austral Land) the sun is obviously a double, clear fire. In this sense the language of real characters is distinguished from the natural languages where, if *month* means a length of time, the relationship between noun and notion (or thing) in both cases is entirely arbitrary. In other terms, if, by mistake, we write *catt*, this does not indicate, say, a cat with an extra leg, whereas, if in the Austral language you write, or say, *icc* instead of *ic*, probably you want to indicate water not hot but boiling hot.

As I said earlier, the system recalls the language of chemical formulas: if you write H_2Au instead of H_2O, in theory you indicate a different chemical compound. But here the first drawback of the system crops up. In chemistry, the system remains, so to speak, open (accommodating neologisms) in case an absolutely new compound has to be named, but the acceptance of the neologism is conditioned by the system of the content. Because in nature the number of known or admitted compounds is limited, one may confidently read H_2Au as a mistake, a misspelling, as it were. But in the Austral language, what happens if ones rungs into the syntagm *al*? Must one admit the possibility that there exists a "wet fire"?

A problem of this sort emerged in connection with the semantic universals that Ramon Lull subjected to combinations and permutations, where the free combination of letters could theoretically produce an utterance repellent to the philosophical bases of the system into which it was introduced (or, in other words, a heretical utterance, such as "truth is false" or "God is lascivious"). But in these cases Lull considered null the theologically unacceptable combination. This also occurred because the letters denoted metaphysical entities that, in the realm of the theology of reference, were precisely defined. *Bonitas est magna* means that Goodness is great, but as Goodness was already defined in this way, it was impossible to conceive of its opposite, *Bonitas est mala* (Goodness is evil). Likewise the *ars* did not contemplate the possibility of metaphorical expressions or even of periphrases. The primitive terms employed defined the entire universe of what was theologically sayable. Lull, with his perfect theological language, was not interested in talking about stars or hot water.

On the contrary, the Austral language uses a very limited battery of primitives but must serve to express every possible experience, that is, to replace through compositions of primitives the entire vocabulary. Thus, as can be seen from the quotation above, it must employ periphrases that, in Foigny's satirical version, are highly questionable metaphors: apple becomes sweet and desirable water, and the act of loving is expressed as *af* (dry fire), or burning derived from the fire of passion. If *dry fire* means love, then why should *wet fire* not be able to mean metaphorically some other thing? The problem that arises, analyzing this caricature of language, is a serious problem: if a few primitives must denominate many things, it is indispensable to recur to periphrasis, and this is precisely what happens with the "serious" projects of Wilkins and Dalgarno. And the confines between periphrasis and metaphorical expression can become very hazy. In fact, in Dalgarno's serious project compounds were introduced on the order of "animal + full-hoofs + spirited" to signify horse and "animal + full-hoofs + huge" to signify elephant.

The equally serious project of Wilkins was based on the fact that all ambiguities of language had to be reduced so that every sign would refer to a single, rigorously defined concept. But some metaphorical operators were introduced to allow the language to express entities for which no terms existed in the philosophical dictionary, whose format had inevitably to be reduced. Wilkins asserts that it is not necessary to have a character for *calf* because the concept can be reached by combining *cow* and *young*; nor does one need a primitive *lioness*, since this animal can be denoted by combining the sign for *female* to that for *lion*. Thus Wilkins develops in his grammar (and then transforms into a system of special signs in the part devoted to the writing and pronunciation of the characters) a system of "Transcendental Particles" intended to amplify or alter the character to which they are applied. The list contemplates eight classes amounting to a total of forty-eight particles, but the criterion that assembles them is not at all systematic. Wilkins harks back to Latin grammar, which makes use of endings/suffixes (that allow the creation of terms like *lucesco, aquosus, homunculus*); of "segregates" such as *tim* and *genus* (allowing the creation, from a root, of *gradatim* or *multigenus*); and determinations of place (hence *vestiarium*) and agent (cf. *arator*). Some of his particles are without doubt of a grammatical nature (for example, those that transform masculine into feminine or adult into young). But Wilkins himself recurs also to the criteria of rhetoric, citing metaphor, synecdoche, and metonymy, and, in fact, the particles in the metaphorical-like category are simply signs of rhetorical interpretation. Thus, adding one of these particles to *root* one gains *original*,

while adding it to *light* yields *evident*. Finally, other particles seem
to refer to the cause-effect relation, or container–thing contained, or function-activity, as in the following examples:

like + *foot* = *pedestal*
like + *blood* = *crimson*
place + *metal* = *mine*
officer + *navy* = *admiral*
artist + *star* = *astronomer*
voice + *lion* = *roar*

From the point of view of linguistic precision, this is the weak-
est part of the project. In fact, Wilkins, who supplies a long list of
examples of the correct application of such particles, warns that
they are, in fact, examples. Therefore the list is open, and its en-
richment depends on the inventiveness of the speaker. It seems almost that Wilkins, concerned about the mechanical quality of his
language, is anxious to leave room for its users' creativity. But once
the user is free to apply these particles to any term, it is obvious
that ambiguity will be hard to avoid.

And so the artificial language loses its one virtue: that of de-
noting always and only the same thing with the same character.

The Austral language (like the models it parodies) deliberately
rejects the fundamental mechanism of every natural language,
namely, double articulation. It is obvious how much double articulation (in which the units of second articulation are without
meaning) can contribute to the free formation of neologisms. If,
with three meaningless characters (p, o, t), I can compose six syn-
tagma (*pot*, *top*, *opt*, *pto*, *otp*, *tpo*), and only three of these are admitted by the dictionary, the other three remain available for constructing neologisms or indicating the most subtle differences
between otherwise similar entities. As long as they remain available, however, if they happen to appear in a context, they may be
understood as errors in pronunciation or spelling.

Foigny's system, on the one hand, allows the creation of neologisms only through metaphor and, on the other, obliges us to seek out a meaning for every syntagm admitted by the *ars combinatoria*, because even the slightest phonetic or orthographic change immediately reflects on the content and denotes a different (and possible) entity.

Finally, the last limitation of the Austral language is—as occurred with many a priori philosophical languages—the absolute casualness with which the primitives are chosen. We will not speak of the so-called Anonymous Spaniard (Pedro Bermudo), who classified the primitives, subdividing them into:

1) Elements (fire, wind, smoke, ash, hell, purgatory, and center of the earth). 2) Celestial entities (stars, lightning, rainbow). 3) Intellectual entities (God, Jesus, discourse, opinion, suspicion, soul, stratagem or specter. 4) Secular states (emperor, barons, plebs). 5) Ecclesiastical states. 6) Artificers (painter or sailor). 7) Instruments. 8) Affects (love, justice, lust). 9) Religion. 10) Sacramental confession. 11) Tribunal. 12) Army. 13) Medicine (doctor, hunger, enema). 14) Brute animals. 15) Birds. 16) Reptiles and fish. 17) Parts of animals. 18) Furnishings. 19) Foods. 20) Beverages and liquids (wine, beer, water, butter, wax, resin). 21) Clothing. 22) Silken stuffs. 23) Woolens. 24) Canvas and other textiles. 25) Navigation and spices (ship, cinnamon, anchor, chocolate). 26) Metals and coins. 27) Various artifacts. 28) Stones. 29) Jewels. 30) Trees and fruits. 31) Public places. 32) Weights and measures. 33) Numerals. 34–42) Various grammatical categories. 43) Persons (pronouns, forms of address such as His Eminence). 44) Travel (hay, road, robber) . . .

but Wilkins himself, though he discussed his list with students of botany, mineralogy, and zoology, put under the heading of Economic Relations not only cases of kinship, in which distinctions appear distorted by criteria such as Progenitor/Descendant, Brother/Half-brother, or *Coelebs*/Virgin (*Coelebs*, however, comprises both the bachelor and the spinster, whereas Virgin seems to refer only to a female condition), but also acts that refer to intersubjective relationships, such as Direct/Seduce or Defense/Desertion. Among the Private Relations appear also Provisions, where we find Butter/Cheese but also Butchering/Cooking and Box/Basket.

Note the sly way that Foigny breaks the homogeneity of the list of the four classic elements by adding salt, which, if anything, would belong to another chemical-alchemistic taxonomy, including also mercury and sulfur. But the slyness is not gratuitous precisely because Wilkins added to the four elements a fifth, evident one: the Meteor.

As for the thirty-six accidentals, even if we know only eighteen of them, their heterogeneity is enough for us to infer that the list has prominent omissions. Here Foigny touches palpably the crucial question of the list of the primitives, and he resolves it more in the manner of the Anonymous Spaniard than in that of Wilkins, but only to insinuate (it seems) that, when it comes to incongruity, there is only a difference of degree between the two systems.

The final comic element in the Austral language is that it does not clarify when a letter has a lexical function or when it is morphemathic. It seems that *l*, *m*, and *p*—placed in the first position—function as pronouns. But, in analyzing *pa* (thou lovest), Foigny speaks of the sweetness of the lover. Thus he assigns to two letters with morphemathic functions the meaning they have when they define accidentals. The solution is comic because it allows us to think that *lu* (I work) must be interpreted with reference to the sweat produced by the earth, but in that case why would there be sweetness in *pu* (thou workest)?

We cannot tell how consciously Foigny was being ironic about the fact that in the philosophical languages the entire grammar is semanticized, but this mischievousness is not to be overlooked.

Criticism of a priori philosophical languages for the most part appears, as I have shown, in French satirical works. Perhaps this is not an accident: it was in France that the first radical criticism of the project took shape in the serious works of Dalgarno, Wilkins, and Lodwick.

In 1629 the Minim friar Marin Mersenne sends his friend

Descartes the project of a *nouvelle langue* by a certain des Vallées. In a letter to Mersenne on 20 November 1629, Descartes sends his impressions of that proposal. For every language, he says, it is necessary to learn a grammar and the meaning of the words. For the meaning of the words it would suffice to have a good dictionary, but the grammar is difficult. Nevertheless, if a grammar could be constructed free of the irregularities of the natural languages, which have been corrupted by use, the problem would be solvable. Thus simplified, this language would appear primitive compared to the others, which would appear as its dialects. And once the primitive terms were set (of which the terms of the other languages would be synonyms, such as *aimer* and *to love*), it would suffice to add the affixes to obtain, for example, the corresponding substantive. Consequently, a system of universal writing could be developed in which every primitive term would be recorded with a number that would refer back to the synonyms in the different languages.

All the same, there would still remain the problem of the sounds to choose for these terms, inasmuch as certain sounds are pleasant and easy for one people and unpleasant for another. The sounds would thus be difficult to learn: if a speaker used synonyms in his own language for the primitive terms, then he would not be understood by speakers of other nations, except in writing. Yet learning the entire lexicon would require great effort, and if that were necessary, there would seem to be no reason not to use an international language already known to many, such as Latin.

Saying this, Descartes only repeated some ideas that were in the air in those decades. But at this point he saw that the central problem is something else altogether: to be able not only to learn but also to remember the primitive nouns, these would have to correspond to an order of ideas, or of thoughts, that would have the same logic as the order of the numbers (where it is not necessary to learn them all but simply to generate them by succession). This problem coincides with another: that of a true philosophy able to define a system of clear and distinct ideas. If a person were able to number all the simple ideas from which are then generated all the ideas that we are capable of thinking and to assign to each of these a character, we could then articulate, as we do with numbers, this sort of mathematics of thought. The words of our languages, on the other hand, refer to confused ideas.

In conclusion, Descartes affirmed: "Now I believe that this language is possible and that the learning on which it depends could be found, by which peasants will be able to judge the truth better than philosophers do now. But I have no faith in ever seeing it used; it presupposes great changes in the order of things, and the whole world would have to be nothing more than an earthly paradise, which can be proposed only in the land of novels."

The criticism of Descartes was correct. Every attempt to establish an architectonically perfect system of ideas composed of mutual dependences and strict classification from the general to the particular would prove to be a failure. At the end of the eighteenth century de Gerando, in *Des signes*, would isolate the secret termite that was gnawing at all the previous systems: either you create a logical dictionary confined to a very limited notional field or an encyclopedia of all our knowledge, that is, either a necessary but insufficient order of concepts or the flexible, infinitely amplifiable and variable order of a library.

On the other hand, Leibniz would acknowledge (in his *Nouveaux essais sur l'entendement humain*) that, having to depict the entire system of our learning, we would have a library where the doctrine of spirits could come under logic but also under morality, and all could come under the practical philosophy to the extent that it contributes to our happiness. A memorable story can be placed in the annals of universal history or in the specific history of a country or even in the biography of an individual. Anyone who is organizing a library often encounters the problem of deciding in which section a book should be cataloged.

So the only thing to do would be to essay a polydimensional encyclopedia (a hypertext, as we would say today). We can almost hear, in advance, the project that would be theorized by D'Alembert at the beginning of the *Encyclopédie*, where he speaks of the

Système Général des Sciences et des Arts as a labyrinth, a tortuous path composed of diverse branches, "some of which converge towards a same center; and since, departing from it, it is not possible to follow all the paths at once, the choice is determined by the nature of the different spirits." The philosopher is he who can discover the secret routes of this labyrinth, its temporary branches, the reciprocal dependences that compose this enclosure like a globe. Consequently, "it is thus possible to imagine as many different systems of human knowledge as there are globes possible of being constructed according to different projections . . . often an object, placed in a given class according one or more of its properties can belong to another class thanks to certain other properties."

The criticism of the *Encyclopédie* puts an end to the dream of the grammar of ideas, even though further attempts would follow, down to our own day, when scholars are still studying the possibility of a so-called *mentalese*, a language written in the very convolutions of our brain, capable of supplying the deep structure of every expression in any natural language.

But as Descartes had announced, it is not impossible to write of ideal languages in the land of novels. Foigny did it, and two and a half centuries later, Borges was to do it, too.

In *Other Inquisitions*, Borges, studying "the language of John Wilkins" (which, by his explicit admission, he knew only through an encyclopedia entry), recognizes at once the incongruity of the classification of the Wilkinsian semantic primitives (he discusses specifically the subdivisions of stones), and it is in this same brief text that he invents the Chinese classification that Foucault quotes at the opening of *Les mots et les choses*. In this Chinese encyclopedia, entitled *Celestial Emporium of Benevolent Recognitions*, "it is written that the animals are divided into (a) those that belong to the Emperor, (b) embalmed ones, (c) those that are trained, (d) suckling pigs, (e) mermaids, (f) fabulous ones, (g) stray dogs, (h) those that are included in this classification, (i) those that tremble as if they were mad, (j) innumerable ones, (k) those drawn with a very fine camel's hair brush, (l) others, (m) those that have just broken a flower vase, (n) those that resemble flies from a distance."[2] Borges comes to the conclusion that no classification in the universe is not arbitrary and conjectural. But if it has to be arbitrary and conjectural, why not leave room not for the satire of utopian projects but for the utopia of linguistic fancy?

Borges, on at least two other occasions, returns to the question of ideal languages. In "Dr. Brodie's Report" he examines the monosyllabic language of the Yahoos.

> Each monosyllabic word corresponds to a general idea whose specific meaning depends on the context or upon accompanying grimaces. The word "nrz," for example, suggests dispersion or spots and may stand for the starry sky, a leopard, a flock of birds, smallpox, something bespattered, the act of scattering, or the flight that follows defeat in warfare. "Hrl," on the other hand, means something compact or dense. It stands for the tribe, a tree trunk, a stone, a heap of stones, the act of heaping stones, the gathering of the four witch-doctors, carnal conjunction or a forest. Pronounced in another manner or accompanied by other grimaces, each word may hold an opposite meaning.[3]

This language of the Yahoos is not at all impracticable, as it seems at first glance. Note that the apparent polysemia of the term is, so to speak, held together by certain primitive special signs common to all its meanings. The grimaces that accompany the emission of sound function like the metaphorical operators of Wilkins. For the rest, the language simply carries to extremes the tendency of actual natural languages to contain expressions that mean different things in different contexts, and Borges hastens to remind his readers that this should not be surprising; after all, in English, *to cleave* means both "to split" and "to cling to."

Finally, in "Tlön, Uqbar, Orbis Tertius" (in *Ficciones*), Borges speaks of a language structured spatially and not temporally, which proceeds not through agglutinations as in the languages so far examined but only by expressing temporal flow. In this language, nouns do not exist, but only impersonal verbs qualified by mono-syllabic suffixes and prefixes with adverbial value. In brief, "there is no word corresponding to the noun *moon*, but there is a verb *to moon* or *to moondle*. *The moon rose over the sea* would thus be writ-ten *hlör u fang axaxaxas mlö*, or, to put it in order: *upward beyond the constant flow there was moondling*" (which suggests some passage in Joyce's *Finnegans Wake*).[4]

The failure of the utopias of the a priori philosophical language has thus produced some interesting experiments in the Land of Novels that, instead of constructing perfect linguistic systems, have demonstrated how our imperfect languages can produce texts en-dowed with some poetic virtue or some visionary force. I consider this no small achievement.

5 | THE LINGUISTICS OF JOSEPH DE MAISTRE

In the story of the centuries-long search for a perfect language, a central chapter should be devoted to the rediscovery of a series of matrix languages or of a primordial mother tongue. For many centuries, the leading claimant for the position of mother tongue was Hebrew. Then other candidates would appear on the scene (Chinese, for example), and finally the search would lose its utopian fervor and its mystical tension as the science of linguistics was born and, with it, the Indo-European hypothesis. For a long time, though, the idea of a primigenial language not only had a historical validity (to rediscover the speech of all mankind before the confusion of Babel) but also a semantic one. In fact, this primigenial language should incorporate a natural relationship between words and things. The primigenial language also had revelatory value for, in speaking it, the speaker would recognize the nature of the named reality.

This tendency, which Genette has called "mimologism,"[1] has an ancient and distinguished ancestry in Western tradition, its prime example being the *Cratylus* of Plato. The idea—already contested in the two previous centuries through the hypotheses known as "epicurean" and polygenetic—underwent a crisis in what Rosiello would have called "enlightened linguistics."[2] But this crisis occurred at the level of the official (which is another way of saying victorious) philosophical and linguistic culture, and the notion survived in many mystical and philosophical trends and has resurfaced even today in the work of those whom the nineteenth-century French tradition had begun calling *les fous du langage.*

I am indebted to Andrew White for some suggestions on the way the mystical version of the monogenetic hypothesis was prolonged in the theosophical ambience of the late eighteenth century (in Louis-Claude de Saint Martin, *De l'ésprit des choses,* for example) and among the French Catholic legitimists such as De Bonald (*Récherches philosophiques*) and Lamennais (*Essai sur l'indifférence en matière de religion*).[3] White also quoted Joseph de Maistre, an alluring clue, because Maistre represents a fusion of the themes of classic legitimism (of which he can be considered the initiator) and those of the theosophism hovering in the circles of Scottish and Templar masonry to which Maistre had at first belonged, though he broke with them for reasons of religious orthodoxy (reaffirming the authority of the Church and the pope against that of any clique of Illuminati).

In a debate on the subject, Raffaele Simone suggested that much of the search for a perfect language derived from a sort of neurotic uneasiness, because people would like to find in words an expression of the way the world works, and they are regularly disappointed. This is certainly true. In the legitimist tradition, the assertion of the sacrality of language aims not so much at reconstructing a primigenial language as at rediscovering the traces of our natural languages. The intent is first of all to question the materialistic claims of all the epicurean, polygenetic hypotheses and then to reject every conventionalist theory as a way of separating language from the very source of Truth.

Since it is linguistically difficult to demonstrate that a relationship exists between words and the essence of things (not least because of the plurality of languages), the way followed by the monogeneticists does not differ much from that of the most fanciful etymologists of the past, Isidore of Seville at their head. The fact that many of these etymologies also reappear in some contemporary thought (in Heidegger, for example) only indicates the toughness of the dream, or perhaps an irrepressible need to have some contact with Being.

If we take a look at the text in which Maistre discussed at great-est length the nature of languages, his *Soirées de Saint-Pétersbourg,* we see that the first declarations simply repropose what is found even today among authors who hark back to tradition as the source of all knowledge, opposing the degenerate learning of a secularized culture, "modern," "enlightened," or "scientistic."[4]

> Listen to wise antiquity on the subject of the first men; it will tell you that they were wondrous and that beings of a higher order deigned to favor them with the most precious of revelations. On this point all agree, the initiates, the philosophers, the poets, history, legend: Asia and Europe have a sole voice. This accord among reason, Revelation, and all human traditions represents such a demonstration that it can be contradicted only in words. Men therefore have not only begun with science but with a science different from ours and superior to it, because it began at a higher level, making it also very dangerous. And this explains why science, at its begin-nings, remained closed within the temples, where finally it became extinguished when this flame could serve no purpose save to burn. (97–98)

But just when readers might expect proof of this theory, they always find themselves confronted by inconsistent, circular argu-ments. Maistre recalls that Julian the Apostate in one of his dis-courses called the sun "the seven-rayed god," and he wonders where the emperor found such a singular attribute. His answer is that the idea could have come to him only from the ancient Asi-atic tradition to which he recurred in his theurgic renovation. Maistre cites, for example, "the sacred books of India," which speak of seven virgins gathered to celebrate the advent of Krishna when the god suddenly appears to them, inviting them to dance. When the virgins object that they have no dancing partners, the god di-vides himself into seven, giving each virgin her own Krishna.

There is really nothing so strange about Julian's choice of

imagery, inasmuch as the hebdomad, the mystique of the number seven, is found in many ancient cultures, and Julian could have absorbed it either from Indian sources or from others. But what indicates a strange disjuncture of thought is the series of examples that follows hard upon Maistre's evocation of Julian: First of all, he notes, the "true" system of the universe was known from most remote antiquity, as is shown by the pyramids of Egypt, which are rigorously oriented according to astronomical criteria. Then, whether as proof or consequence of this fact, we observe that a people like the Egyptians, who could create colors that have lasted thirty centuries, raise boulders against every law of mechanics to a height of six hundred feet, carve in granite birds of all known species, could hardly fail to excel in every other art, and therefore they must have known things of which we are ignorant. Finally, in Asia, consider the ancient astronomical observations carved on the walls of Nimrud, which rose on land still damp from the Flood. All this drives one—notice the conclusion—to ask oneself, "Where will we collocate then the so-called eras of barbarism and ignorance?" (101–102).

We cannot see a direct rapport between the metaphor of the seven rays and the pyramids, unless it is to be found in the fact that different myths and archetypes tried to explain astronomical phenomena and furnished a pre-Galilean version of a world written in mathematical characters. But to confirm the existence of these trends Plato would again suffice, with his *Timaeus*. If anything, it is the knowledge that even more ancient images circulated in African and Asian culture that explains why Julian followed this tradition. Whether he followed it or revitalized it, however, this does not show that he was its direct and authorized heir or that the tradition spoke any truth.

But this reasoning had been typical of the same Masonic tradition that influenced Maistre: the fact that an association decided to hark back to the Templar tradition became a sign of direct descent.

It is obvious that in this reasoning there is no linguistic-etymological discovery, but only biased polemic against sick modern civilization: "Under the tight dress of the north, its head stifled by the curls of false hair, arms laden with books and instruments of every kind, pale from vigils and labor, it draws itself on, ink-stained and out of breath, along the path of truth, lowering always its brow, furrowed by algebraic formulas" (104). Compared to that of our modern civilization, the knowledge of the origins reveals its obvious superiority:

> As far as it is possible to observe the science of the primitive ages, despite the enormous distance, we see it always free, independent; it does not so much walk as fly, and in all its bearing there is something aerial and supernatural. It flings its hair to the wind, beneath an Oriental miter. The *efod* covers its bosom; lifted by inspiration, it looks only at the sky; and its scornful foot seems to touch the earth only to detach itself from it. Although this primitive science never asked anything of anyone, and relied on no human support, we still have proof that it possessed the most rare kinds of knowledge.
>
> (104–105)

The proof of this primacy would lie in the fact that traditional science was exempted from the task imposed on modern science, while all the calculations that we base on experimentation are the most false that can be imagined. Whence we see that the thesis—demonstrate that modern civilization is inferior to ancient civilization—is reasserted as proof.

At this point the Greek myth of the golden age is proposed as proof that the state of perfect and luminous knowledge existed only in the civilizations of the origins (107). Thus the man who had written pages, truly beautiful from a literary point of view, on the revolution's crime, rediscovers the root of every Jacobin degradation in the act (so remote that it can no longer be collocated in history) with which language fell away from the original tree (108).

Seekers after original Hebrew, even if they could retrace its origin only into a past Eden (of which they had to make an effort, moreover, to offer, however fancifully, a chronology) did not therefore refrain from reconstructing its grammar. Compared with the efforts of a man such as Father Kircher to decipher Egyptian hieroglyphics and study the generating of alphabets, the efforts of Maistre seem fairly puerile: "Here is the mystery, gentlemen: one generation said *ba*, the other said *be*; the Assyrians invented the nominative, and the Medes, the genitive" (116)—which, if anything, would be proof not of a divine origin of languages but precisely of their slow evolution. Maistre asks himself why, in the languages of the ancient peoples, we find reflections of knowledge that those people could not have possessed. The correct question naturally would not be "why" but "whether." In fact, Maistre goes on to illustrate not inconceivable knowledge but proofs of the fact, common among ancients as among moderns, that poets are capable of finding ingenious metaphors to name phenomena fundamental to human experience.

For example, where, at least three thousand years ago, did the Greeks find the attribute of *phisizoos* (that which gives, or possesses life), that Homer applies at times to the earth? Or, its near synonym, *pheresbios*, which Hesiod uses in the same context? Where did they find the even more singular attribute, *philemate* (loving, or thirsting for blood), which is given to the same earth in a tragedy? Who taught the Greeks to call sulphur "divine," as it is the sign of fire? I am no less amazed by the noun *cosmos*, given to the world. The Greeks called it *beauty* because "all order is beautiful," which we then also adopted, changing only the desinence. The Greek term excludes disorder, whereas the Latin one excludes impurity: still at bottom there is the same idea, and the two terms are both correct and both false. Further, I beg you, explain this other matter to me: how could the ancient Latins, when they knew only how to fight wars and plow fields, imagine that with the same term they were expressing the idea of prayer

and that of punishment? Who taught them to call fever "pu-
rifying" or "expiating"? Are we perhaps dealing with a judg-
ment, a genuine awareness, through which a people affirms
the exactness of a term? But do you believe that judgments
of this sort could have been formulated in a period when
people barely knew how to write, when a dictator tilled his
own field, when they wrote verses that Varro and Cicero already could no longer understand? These words, and many
others that could be abundantly cited, found in all Oriental
metaphysics, are obvious remains of more ancient languages,
erased or forgotten. (117–119)

Here we are simply demonstrating that every epoch had its poets,
capable of naming things in an unusual and perspicacious fashion. Or, at most, we are repeating, in a simplified form, a thesis
inspired by Vico on the metaphoric origin of language that is, if
anything, a reflection of the perceptive freshness of ancient peoples, not of their presumed occult knowledge. It hardly seems
that any profound learning was necessary for agrarian peoples to
call the earth "life-giving" as they lived, in fact, on the earth's
fruits.

Maistre was a vigorous thinker, capable of historically based critical judgments (it suffices to look at his contestations of the Templar myth of the Scottish masonry). And he was not ignorant of the
attempts made to construct an a priori philosophical language, from
Bacon to Wilkins and beyond. He perceives the contrivances of the
artificial languages proposed in the course of the previous two centuries, to which common sense would reply that natural languages
seem more flexible in handling our experience. But then this position (which, thus enunciated, would prove disastrously "enlightened") in Maistre's discourse is radically transformed. To demonstrate the agility of natural languages Maistre cannot avoid
recurring to another notion, born in the eighteenth century: that
of the "genius" of languages. But the notion of genius recalls that of
polygenesis, or at least of autonomous development, unreconcilable

with any monogenetic hypothesis. Maistre thus finds himself entangled in a line of reasoning that leads to wild paralogisms:

> I would like, however, to underline a fact, whose obviousness is undeniable, namely, the prodigious talent demonstrated by young peoples in forming words and, on the other hand, the absolute inability of philosophers to do the same, in the most refined centuries. I recall that Plato already points out this talent of peoples in their infancy. What is amazing is that they give the impression of having followed deliberate criteria, thanks to a precise system of agreement, despite the fact that this was from any viewpoint strictly impossible. Every language has its genius, a genius that is unique, therefore we must exclude any idea of composition, of arbitrary formation, and of antecedent convention. (120–121)

The notion of genius does not exclude convention, unless the former is understood as a kind of mystical insufflation that comes from outside the linguistic formative process. Maistre decides to isolate the "genius" specific to Greek and to Latin in some morphological characteristics of the two languages, an admissible method, without making any decision as to the precision of the analysis. Thus he observes that in Greek compound words can be formed, in which the two parts generate a second meaning, without therewith becoming unrecognizable, whereas Latin tends to shatter the words in such a way that from their fragments, chosen and joined through some unknown and quite singular agglutinations, are born new words of surprising beauty, whose elements are no longer recognizable except to a trained eye (121). But here is the proof:

> from these three words, *CAro DAta VERmibus* they have formed the word *CA-DA-VER*, "meat abandoned to the worms." From two other words, *MAgis* and *voLO*, they have made *MALO* and *NOLO*, two splendid verbs that every language, Greek included, can envy Latin. . . . The French have

not totally ignored this system. For example, to give a name to those who were our ancestors, they formed the word *AN-CETRE*, joining part of the word *ANCien* [old, ancient] with the verb *ETRE* [to be], just as they formed the term *BEF-FROI* [alarm bell], joining *Bel* [beautiful] and *EFFROI* [fright]. You see then how they utilized the two terms *DUo* and *IRE* to form the verb *DUIRE*, [to go in a pair] and, through natural extension of the verb *condurre* [conduct, lead], *diriger* [direct]. With the personal pronoun *SE*, with the relative adverb of place *HORS* [outside] and with the verbal ending *TIR*, they formed *S-OR-TIR* [to go out], that is, *SE-HORS-TIR* "to put one's own person outside the place where it was." All this to me seems wondrous. (121–123)

This passage displays two contradictions. In the first part, the fact that two languages evolved through different morphological rules is, if anything (as we have said), an argument against monogenetism. In the second part, with a specific quotation from Isidore, Maistre tries to play the etymological card. But at least the etymology of the seventeenth-century monogenesists consisted of showing how the words of each language had developed from a single Hebrew root (the only one, for that matter, to have a presumed "iconic" or motivated relationship with the thing signified). Here, on the contrary, the game consists of demonstrating that within each language, and with quite different mechanisms, compound words can be created whose meanings are born from the sum of the meanings of their simple components, which is what happens in the natural languages when they compose terms like *screwdriver, corkscrew, parasol* or when spontaneous agglutinations are born, as in the transformation of Medio-lanum into Milan—though, alas, this never happened with the Latin word *cadaver*. Even if Isidore's etymology of *cadaver* were plausible, and even if *beffroi* had the etymology attributed to it by Maistre, this would in no way prove any iconic and motivated relation between simple words and signified reality but rather, if anything, that new coinages are often born from the wordplay typical of the rhetors of decadence and not from an instinctive folk wisdom.

The fact that this aspect could escape Maistre is explained only by the religious—and not linguistic—exigency that he convince his readers (almost pedagogically) that language says originally the Truth. And we sense this from some expressions of outright joy with which he glimpses the action, within every human language, of this impulse to tell always the truth, no matter what: "It is a pleasure to witness, so to speak, the action of this hidden principle that forms languages. Sometimes we see it struggling against a difficulty that arrests it on its path: it seeks a form that is lacking, the materials at its disposal resist; then it will solve the problem with a happy solecism and will say, very effectively, 'rue passante,' 'couleur voyante,' 'place marchande,' 'métal cassant,' etc." (125).

No objection would be made as to the efficacy of these compounds, were it not for the fact that Maistre is not always fond of compounds (or of the hidden action a language forms in order to mint them), as if a language, in some of its vicissitudes, remained faithful to its own obligation to truth and in other instances degenerated. As examples of degeneration, he cites the fact that already in his own day (and in the St. Petersburg familiar to him) on visiting cards one could find titles such as *Minister, Général, Kammerherr, Fraülein, Général-Anchef, Général-Dejournei, Joustizii-Minister*, and that on commercial posters words like *magazei, fabrica, meubel*, or that in the course of military drills commands were heard such as *directii na prava, na leva, deployade en échiquier, en échelon, contre-marche*, or that in the army functions should be named *haupt-wacht, exercise hause, ordonnance-hause, commisariat, cazarma, canzellarii*.

Immediately afterward, he mentions terms considered "beautiful, elegant, and expressive" that presumably existed in "your primitive language": *souproug* (bridegroom), which precisely means "he who is attached with another to a single yoke," and he comments that "nothing more correct or more inspired" could have been found, just as "we must admit that the savages or the barbarians who once deliberated to form such nouns surely did not lack refinement" (127).

It is obvious that there is no reason (except the imponderable one of taste) to decide that *place marchande* is legitimate and *contremarche* is not. It is unclear why to describe the bridegroom as someone attached to the same yoke (which could be simply a carnival taunt) seems beautiful, whereas it is horrible to give an order for an army to deploy itself like a chessboard (an effective spatial metaphor). Perhaps here Maistre laments only the introduction of barbarisms and therefore the pollution of one language with terms borrowed from another. In any case, he seems to react according to his personal stylistic preferences, "by ear."

The point is that, if language must be considered the only way to enter into a rapport with the Sacred, every etymology must be "good"; in every metaphor, even the most banal, there should shine a truth, even in *screwdriver*. Since *rue passante* is not sufficiently ancient to belong to the golden age, in recognizing it as an undegenerate expression Maistre is simply privileging the freshness of popular language over that of bureaucratic language. If he were to trace these and other discriminants, he would shift from mystical linguistics to sociolinguistics, an intention that is very far from his mind.

In fact, he returns constantly to the idea that the perfect language is that of the origins:

> The formation of the most perfected words, the most meaningful, the most philosophical, in the fullest sense of the word, occurs unfailingly in periods of ignorance and simplicity. . . . The "onomathurgical" talent is invariably disappearing as we descend toward the civilized and scientific eras. In all the writings that appear in our time on this most interesting subject, there is nothing but an invocation of a "philosophical language" without knowing, indeed without even suspecting, that the most philosophical language is that in which philosophy is least mingled. The latter lacks two little faculties necessary to create words: intelligence to invent them and au-

thority to have them adopted. Does philosophy see a new object? It will go and leaf through its dictionaries to find an ancient or foreign term, and almost always the enterprise comes to a bad end. *Montgolfière*, for example, which is used throughout the country, is correct, at least in one sense, and I prefer it to *areòstate*, which is a scientific term but suggests nothing: you could just as well call a ship a *hydrostate*. Observe the invasion of new words borrowed from the Greek over the last twenty years, gradually, as crimes or madness demanded them: more or less all of them are formed erroneously, they are self-contradictory. *Theophilanthropist*, for example, is a term more foolish than the thing in itself, which is saying plenty; a simple English or German scholar would have been led to say, on the contrary, *Theanthpophile*. You will reply that this word was invented by wretches in a wretched age, and yet the terminology of chemistry, which was surely created by enlightened men, begins precisely with the lowest sort of solecism—*oxygen*—when they should say instead *oxygon*. I am not a chemist, but I have excellent reasons to believe that all this terminology is destined to vanish; the fact remains, in any case, that from a philological and grammatical point of view, it would be the most unhappy imaginable, if the prize for barbarism were not contested and wrested away by the metric vocabulary. (138–140)

Why should *oxygen* be more unhappy than the very unhappy *oxygon*? This is what Maistre does not explain. If language is seen as what the world was for the Middle Ages, as a natural revelation of Truth, nothing in language should be wrong. As medieval thinkers said, even monsters should show the power of God. Furthermore, as Maistre is the first to assert, in language there is a glottogonic force that overcomes all human resistance (and hence language is always right).

It must, however, be said that, at least in one case, Maistre's reasoning finds a logically plausible formulation. He seeks, in effect, to distinguish three concepts: (1) the historical paternity through which every language derives from another, all tracing their ancestry back to the same, primigenial source; (2) the autonomous force whereby every language develops its own genius, and (3) the presence within each language of a "superlinguistic" force, a sort of divinely bestowed *energheia* that causes, within each language, without necessarily any historical descendance or borrowing, the same miracle of the primordial language to take place. Thus the following passage becomes comprehensible, as it denies thesis 1 in the first paragraph and affirms thesis 2 in the second:

> What can be said of the surprising analogies to be found among languages distant from one another in time and space, thus guaranteeing that any possible contact between them is impossible?
>
> (i) Bear in mind that I do not refer to the simple resemblances found among words that the language has acquired simply through contacts or communications.
>
> (ii) I speak only of the similarity of ideas, proved by words that are synonyms as to meaning, *but different in form: thus excluding any idea of borrowing* [emphasis mine]. I will confine myself to pointing out a quite singular case: when it was a question of expressing some idea that in its natural expression could have proved indelicate, the French were often able to find the same paraphrases already used by the Greeks in their day to avoid indecent words, which may seem even more extraordinary if you reflect that, in this respect, the French acted on their own, seeking nothing from their usual intermediaries, the Latins. (127–129)

But after the assertion that every language resolves its own problems by itself, thesis 3 emerges, which sets out to prove that it is no longer a language's autonomy but rather the existence of an original and divine force, the Word, that becomes the source of every language.

If our century has not succeeded in discovering the truth about the origin of language, as about many other questions, the reason is that it was mortally afraid of discovering it. Languages had a beginning, but the word, never, not even with man. It necessarily preceded languages; words, in fact, derive directly from The WORD. Every language is born, like an animal, through an explosion and a development, without man's ever having passed from a state of "aphony" to the use of the word. Man has always spoken, and if the Jews defined man as "speaking animal," they did so for a sublime reason.

(131–132)

But then, immediately afterward, and without a break, thesis 1, rejected in the first paragraph, is reproposed:

When a new language is formed, it is born in the bosom of a society that already has a complete mastery of language, and the action or principle that presides over this formation cannot arbitrarily invent any word; it uses only those that it finds around itself or *that it summons from farther off* [emphasis mine]; it feeds on them, grinds them, digests them, and never adopts them without having altered them, greatly or slightly.

(132)

Finally, to underline the (always good) naturalness with which each single language, grinding or digesting previous elements, forms always suitable words, there is a gloss: "There has been much talk of arbitrary signs in a century in which people have grown passionate about every coarse expression that would exclude order and intelligence, but arbitrary signs do not exist, and every word has its own reason" (132–133). This negates what was previously asserted, namely, that having invented *oxygen* was a sign of degeneration. In fact, Maistre is biased: he thinks (from the beginning) that the modern inventors of *oxygen* were degenerate (inasmuch as they were modern), while the ancient inventors of *cadaver* were right (inasmuch as they were ancient). He is not seized by the suspicion that not even the ancient inventors of *cadaver* were the original Name Giver.

However, we also accept the proposition according to which languages live on borrowings; they transform and adapt, and yet their every word is natural and motivated. If Maistre returned to his example of *rue passante*, he would find that there is a motivation for the compound, but he would not be able to explain the motivation of *rue* and of *passer*, unless he repeated all the contortions of the classic etymologists. Thus, arriving at the crucial point, he gives up. Or, rather, he probably believes that he is not giving up, if the following passage is the expected demonstration. But the total mutual contradiction of the provided examples forces us—in the interest of the reader—to mark within the passage the various theses (all in disagreement among themselves) that it demonstrates. In our view, the theses are the following:

1. *Thesis of obscure borrowing.* Sometimes in a language there existed a word that then somehow passed into another language, which abandoned it but passed it on to a local dialect; for this reason, we may find in an Alpine locality a word used today in the Slavic area. This thesis, however, does not explain why words must reflect the nature of things, nor does it say that they do reflect it.

2. *Thesis of autonomous invention.* Sometimes a word is invented by analogy with a foreign term, sometimes by metaphor. Then each language invents its own terms and does so following quite different criteria.

3. *Thesis of original iconism.* A language does not invent words; it finds them already made, in accord with nature. (No proofs follow.)

4. *Thesis of evident and multiple borrowing.* One language borrows words from different languages, for the widest variety of reasons.

This is how, without a break, four mutually incompatible theses are affirmed.

[*Thesis of obscure borrowing*] You recall perhaps that in this country bran (in Latin *furfur*) is called *Bren*. On the other side of the Alps the civet owl is called *Saca*. If you were asked why the two peoples chose these two phonetic expressions to express the two ideas, you might perhaps be tempted to reply: "Because they felt like it; these are arbitrary choices." And you would be mistaken: in fact, the first of those two words is English and the second Slavic, and from Ragusa to the Kamchatka it retains, in the beautiful Russian language, the same meaning it has eight hundred leagues from here, in a local dialect. You would not affirm, I hope, that men gathered in a council on the Thames, on the Rhine, on the Ob, or on the Po, found by pure chance the same sounds to express the same ideas. The two words already existed in the two languages, and these languages subsequently donated them to the two dialects. Would you maintain that the four races inherited them from an earlier race? I do not believe so, and yet, I admit, it emerges first of all that the two immense families, the Teutonic and the Slavic, did not arbitrarily invent these two words but received them from others. At this point the same problem arises with regard to the antecedent nations: where did they get these words from? And in this case, too, we must reply that they learned them from others, and so we go back in time to the origin of all things.   (133–134)

[*Thesis of autonomous invention*] The candles that are being brought in to us at this moment make me think of their name in French: *bougies*. At one time the French were engaged in great commerce with the city of Botzia in the kingdom of Fez; they imported from there a large quantity of wax candles, which they began to call *botzies*. The national genius very quickly transformed this term and produced *bougies*. The English has retained the ancient expression *wax candles*, whereas the German prefers to say *Wachslicht*. In every case, however, you can rediscover the reason that originated the term. If I had not found the etymology of the word *bougie* in the preface to Thomassin's Hebrew dictionary, where I would never have deliberately looked for it, would I have been less certain of any etymology? To doubt it, the flame of analogy would have to be extinguished: one would have to renounce reason. (134–135)

[*Thesis of original iconism*] Observe, if you please, the very word *etymology*. It is itself a great proof of the prodigious talent of antiquity in discovering or adapting the most perfect words: it presupposes, in fact, that every word is true, that is to say, not arbitrarily imagined, which is already enough to orient an upright spirit. The things that we know on this point are very enlightening. . . . An arbitrary sound has never expressed an idea, nor has it ever been able to. As thought necessarily exists before words, which are only the exterior expression of that thought, so words exist before the flowering of every new language, which receives them as they are, then alters them as it pleases. The genius of each language roams like an animal that wishes to unearth, wherever it may be, what best suits him. (135–136)

[*Thesis of evident and multiple borrowing*] In our French language, for example, *maison* is of Celtic derivation, *palais* is Latin, *basilique* is Greek, *rabot* is Slavic, *honnir* is Teutonic, *almanach* is Arabic, and *sopha* is Hebrew. From where did all this come? It is not really important to know that, at least for the moment; it suffices for me to demonstrate to you that languages are formed only from other languages, which they kill normally to feed on them, like carnivorous animals. (136–137)

The passage concludes: "Let us never speak then of 'chance' or of arbitrary signs" (137). Yet, on the contrary, all the arguments that have gone before seem to militate in favor of a supreme arbitrariness of decisions on the part of the languages. And we are puzzled by the question "Where did all this come from?" which insinuates the idea of a deep source of words. We have just been told where they come from: Celtic, Greek, Latin, Arabic, Turkish, Hebrew.

We have said that the four theses contemporaneously enunciated are not compatible. We will be more specific: all together, they are not compatible with a *strong* idea of the birth and development of languages, but they would be compatible if we admitted that languages are a historical-cultural phenomenon, that they grow without an order decided by a supernatural will, and that they gradually arrive at their stability through borrowings (deliberate or unconscious), poetic inventions, conventional whims and "iconic" attempts. But in this case languages would achieve their organic condition just as, from an evolutionist perspective devoid of any idea of providence, only giraffes would survive in certain conditions because they have the longest necks.

This is what Maistre cannot accept. And this is how he then concludes his linguistic excursus: with a series of thoughts, each of them perhaps acceptable, though when taken all together they seem a fireworks display of non sequiturs.

If you wish me to express myself in another fashion, I will say that the word is eternal, whereas a language is as old as the nation that speaks it. You rebut, without giving the matter enough thought, that no nation can understand any longer its own ancient language. But, pray, what importance does that have? Does change that does not affect principle perhaps destroy identity? Would someone who saw me in my cradle perhaps recognize me today? And yet I believe I am entitled to say I am the same being I was then. And so it is with a language: a language is always the same, as long as the people that speaks it is the same. The poverty of languages at their beginnings is another supposition imposed by all the force and authority of philosophy. New words prove nothing, because, gradually, as the language acquires them, it drops others, and we do not know in what proportion. The only certainty is that every people has spoken, and has spoken precisely insofar as it thought and as it thought; in fact, it would be absurd to believe that there is a sign for a nonexistent concept, as it would be absurd to believe a concept does not have a sign to make itself known. (141–142)

It is true that the *Soirées* record conversations, but surely in this philosophical dialogue Maistre did not wish to give the impression of inconclusive chatter. The lack of conclusion, the iron chain of non sequiturs, reveals a method, not an interlocutory lapse.

For that matter, Maistre himself said as much. Look again at the passage entitled *Thesis of autonomous invention*, and you will see that, in order to believe in etymologies, the "flame of analogy" must not be extinguished, reasoning must not be renounced. This is Maistre's idea of Reason: to reason means to entrust oneself to any analogy that establishes an unbroken network of contacts between every thing and every other thing. This can be said, and it must be done, because it has been assumed that this network has existed since the Origin; indeed, it is itself the basis of all knowledge.

It is typical of reactionary thought to establish a double equation, between Truth and Origin and between Origin and Language. The Thought of Tradition serves only to confirm a mystical belief that arrests any further reasoning.

NOTES |

TRANSLATOR'S NOTE: Unless otherwise noted, the passages quoted in the text are Umberto Eco's translations into English of the originals or my translations into English from his translations into Italian.

1 | THE FORCE OF FALSITY

1. Jeffrey Burton Russell, *Inventing the Flat Earth* (New York: Greenwood, 1991).
2. J. L. E. Dreyer, *History of Planetary Systems from Thales to Kepler* (Princeton: Princeton University Press, 1906); E. J. Dijksterhuis, *The Mechanization of the World Picture* (1950; trans. Oxford: Oxford University Press, 1961)
3. Andrew Dickson White, *History of the Warfare of Science with Theology in Christendom*, 2 vols. (New York: Appleton, 1896).
4. Charles Singer, ed., *Studies in the History and Method of Science* (Oxford: Clarendon Press, 1917–1921); A. Holt-Jensen, *Geography: Its History and Concepts* (London, 1988); Daniel Boorstin, *The Discoverers* (New York: Random House, 1983).
5. See also, for the considerations that follow, Gioia Zaganelli, *La lettera di Prete Gianni* (Parma: Pratiche, 1990).
6. Cf. Umberto Eco, "Fakes and Forgeries," in *The Limits of Interpretation* (Bloomington: Indiana University Press, 1990).
7. Frances Yates, *The Rosicrucian Enlightenment* (London: Routledge and Kegan Paul, 1972).
8. Jorge Luis Borges, "Tlön, Uqbar, Orbis Tertius," *Ficciones*, ed. Anthony Kerrigan (New York: Grove Press, 1962), 21–22, 21.

9. I am well aware that I retold this story in both *Foucault's Pendulum* and *Six Walks*, but it is always a good idea to repeat it, and unfortunately it can never be repeated enough. As always, the information, apart from some personal excursions into the world of the *roman feuilleton*, derives in great part from Norman Cohn's *Warrant for a Genocide* (New York: Harper, 1967) and from that inexhaustible store of anti-Semite arguments, Nesta Weber's *Secret Societies and Subversive Movements* (London: Boswell, 1924).

10. Karl Popper, *Conjectures and Refutations* (London: Routledge, 1969).

11. Arles: Actes Sud, 1994.

2 | LANGUAGES IN PARADISE

1. See my *Search for the Perfect Language* (Oxford: Blackwell, 1995).

2. Maria Corti, *Dante a un nuovo crocevia* (Florence: Libreria Commissionaria Sansoni, 1981).

3. Naturally, English-language readers must remember that *I* in Italian is not a personal pronoun and can at most be read as a plural article (corresponding to *the*). But to the ear of Italian readers, in this context, it does not sound as such.

4. Moshe Idel, *Language, Torah, and Hermeneutics in Abraham Abulafia* (Albany: SUNY Press, 1989).

5. *Sefer* or *ha-Sekhel*, in ibid., 14.

6. Moshe Idel, *The Mystical Experience of Abraham Abulafia* (Albany: SUNY Press, 1988), 21.

7. Idel, *Language, Torah*, 102

8. Jacqueline Genot-Bismuth, "'Pommes d'or masquées d'argent': Les sonnets italiens de Manoel Giudeo (Immanuel de Rome)," Paris.

9. Le Goff, *La civilisation de l'Occident médiéval* (Paris: Arthaud, 1964), 373.

3 | FROM MARCO POLO TO LEIBNIZ

1. Jean-François Champollion, *Lettre à Dacier* (Paris: Didot, 1822), 11–12.

2. *The Bestiary*, ed. T. H. White (New York: Putnam's, 1960), 117–118.

3. Athanasius Kircher, *Obeliscus Pamphilius* (Rome: Grigani, 1650) II, 5, 114–120.

4. Champollion, *Lettre à Dacier*, 29.

5. John Wilkins, *Mercury; or, The Secret and Swift Messenger* (London: Printed by I. Norton, for John Maynard and Timothy Wilkens, 1641), 107.

4 | THE LANGUAGE OF THE AUSTRAL LAND

1. Estienne Guichard, *L'Harmonie étymologique des langues* (Paris: Le Noir, 1610), 147.
2. Jorge Luis Borges, "The Analytical Language of John Wilkins," *Other Inquisitions, 1937–1952*, trans. Ruth L. C. Simms (Austin: University of Texas Press, 1964), 103.
3. "Doctor Brodie's Report," in *Doctor Brodie's Report*, trans. Norman Thomas di Giovanni (London: Penguin, 1976), 97.
4. Borges, "Tlön, Uqbar, Orbis Tertius," *Ficciones* (New York: Grove Press, 1962),

5 | THE LINGUISTICS OF JOSEPH DE MAISTRE

1. Gérard Genette, *Mimologiques* (Paris: Seuil, 1976).
2. Luigi Rosiello, *Linguistica illuminista* (Bologna: Mulino, 1976).
3. Andrew D. White, *A History of the Warfare of Science with Theology in Christendom* (New York: Appleton, 1917) 2:189–208.
4. In the citations from Maistre that follow, the numbers refer to pages in the original edition published by the Librairie Grecque in Paris in 1821.

INDEX |

Abulafia, Abraham ben Samuel,
46–51
accidentals, 81, 90
Acosta, José de, 67
Active Intellect, 46, 48
Adam, viii, 39, 46–47, 51, 55, 77,
79; animals named by, 23,
24–25, 28, 36; Dante and,
34–37, 41–42, 45
Adamic language, 26, 30, 45, 51,
54, 61, 77, 79. *See also* language,
perfect
Aelian (Claudius Aelianus), 59–60
African cultures, 53, 100
agglutinations, 105
d'Ailly, Pierre, 6
Albertus Magnus, 6–7
Alciati, Andrea, 58–59
Alcibiades (Plato), 60
Alembert, Jean Le Rond de, 14,
67, 92–93
Ambrose, Saint, 6, 59
Amerindian cultures, 53, 67–68
amorc (Anticus and Mysticus
Ordo Rosae Crucis), 11
Andrae, Johann Valentin, 10–12
animal naming, 23, 24–25, 28,
54–55, 87, 93, 94

Anonymous Spaniard (Pedro
Bermudo), 89–90
Apperley, Charles James. *See*
Nimrod
Apries (pharaoh), 62
Aquinas. *See* Thomas Aquinas
Archimedes, 5
Aristarchus, 5
Aristophanes, 60
Aristotelianism, 39, 46
Aristotle, 5, 27, 60
Arout, François Marie. *See* Voltaire
Ars Signorum (Dalgarno), 81
Asian culture, 100. *See also* China
astronomy, 18, 62, 100
Augustine, Saint, 6–7, 27–28
Auracepit na n-Éces (precepts of
poets), 28
Austral language, 80–90. *See also*
Foigny, Gabriel de
autonomous invention thesis, 111,
112–13, 115
Averroes, 46
*Avertissement pieux et utile des
frères de la Rosée-Croix*
(Neuhaus), 12
background books, 54–55, 60, 69

Bacon, Francis, 63, 66, 78, 103
Bacon, Roger, 6, 39
Baillet, Adrien, 12
Barruel, abbé, 14
Basil, 59
Becher, Joachim, 84
Bergerac, Cyrano de, 80
Bermudo, Pedro (Anonymous
   Spaniard), 89–90
Berry, duc de, 9
Bible, 27, 28, 55; Cotton Bible,
   29; *Genesis,* 23–25, 35; King
   James version, 24–25, 44; Mar-
   tin Luther German translation,
   24; *Psalm 68,* 44; *Psalm 148,*
   36; translations, viii; Vulgate,
   24, 44
The Birds (Aristophanes), 60
Boethius of Dacia, 39
Bonald, Louis-Gabriel-Ambrose
   de, 98
Boorstin, Daniel, 7
Borges, Jorge Luis, 12–13, 93–94
Bournand, François, 15
Bouvet, Joachim, 70, 74
Brahe, Tycho, 3
Buridan, Jean, 6

cabala, 47, 51, 58
Cabala of the Names (Abulafia), 47
cabalism, 79
Caesar Domitian Augustus, 62
Cagliostro, Alessandro, conte di
   (Giuseppe Balsamo), 15
Cambridge Bestiary, 59–61
Campanella, Tommaso (Giovanni
   Domenico), 10

Carbonari (secret society), 14
caricature, 80
Carpine, Pian del (Giovanni de
   Piano Carpini), 9
cartography, 7, 65
*Celestial Emporium of Benevolent
   Recognitions* (Borges), 93
Celsus, 59
Chain of Genies, 62
Champollion, Jean-François,
   56–57, 62
*Character pro notia linguarum uni-
   versalis* (Becher), 84
chemical formulas, 3, 78–80,
   85–86, 88
China, 63–64; animal classifica-
   tion and, 93; hieroglyphs and,
   66–67; ideograms and, 63, 66,
   78; language of, 97; *Oedypus
   Aegyptiacus,* 65. *See also*
   Marco Polo
China Illustrata (Kircher), 65, 66, 68
Christianopolis (Andrae), 10
Cicero, 60
City of the Sun (Campanella), 10
Columbus, Christopher, viii, 4,
   6–7, 74
Common Writing (Lodwick), 81
"Community" (Peirce), 19–20
Condorcet, 14
Confraternity of the Rosy Cross.
   See Rosicrucians
Confucius, 66
Constantine, 7
Constitutions of Anderson, 13
Contra Celsum (Origen), 59
Copernican theory, 17

Corti, Maria, 38–39, 49
Cosmas Indicopleustes, 5, 17–18
cosmology, 20; Ptolomaic system, 3–4, 17–18, 62
counterfeit documents, 9–10
Cratylus (Plato), 27, 97
Cruz, Gaspar da, 63
cultural anthropology, 74–75
cultural interaction modes, 53–54
culture conquest, 53
Cyon, Elie de, 16
Cyrus, King, 68

Dalgarno, George, 78, 81, 87, 90
Daniele, Lionello de Ser, 50
Dante Alighieri, 4, 6, 23, 30–32, 40–43, 48, 49–51, 77, 78; cabalistic tradition, viii; *forma locutionus,* 37–42, 45, 46, 49; Hebrew and, 33–35, 37, 39, 41, 44; illustrious vernacular, 39–41; Jewish influence, 48–51; language comparisons, 30–35, 43–44; *locutio secundaria,* 32, 34; perfect language, viii, 30, 41–42; vernacular languages, 30–35, 37, 40, 44
Darwinian theory, 4–5
De abstinentia (Porphyry), 59
De animalium natura (Aelian), 59–60
De dignitate and augmentis scientiarum (Bacon), 63, 66
De finibus bonorum et malorum (Cicero), 60
De Genesi ad literam libri duodecim (Augustine), 28

De l'ésprit des choses (Saint Martin), 98
De modis significandi (Boethius), 39
De solertia animalium (Plutarch), 60
De Vulgari Eloquentia (Dante), 30–32, 39, 40–42, 50, 77
Democritus, 6
Des signes (Gerando), 92
Descartes, René, 12, 40, 91–93
Dewey, John, 50
Diderot, Denis, 14, 67
Dijksterhuis, E. J., 5
The Discoverers (Boorstin), 7
Divine Comedy (Dante), 23, 30, 33, 42–43, 48; Hebrew translation, 50
Divine Mind, 23
divine symbols, 56
Donation of Constantine, 7–8, 17–18, 20
double articulation, 88
"Dr. Brodie's Report" (Borges), 94
Dreyer, J. L. E., 5
Dreyfus case, 16
Dumas, Alexandre, 16

earth, shape of, 4–7, 18, 20–21
Eddington, Arthur Stanley, 20
Eden, Garden of, 23, 30, 102. *See also* paradise
Effroyables pactions faites entre de diable et les prétendus invisibles (anonymous), 12
Egidius Romanus, 6
Egyptian culture, 53–54, 56, 100

Electra (Sophocles), 60
Emblemata (Alciati), 58–59
encyclopedia, 21; of China, 65; current truth in, 3; improbable country in, 12–13
Encyclopédie (Alembert), 67, 91–92, 92–93
epicurean hypothesis, 77, 97–98
Epistula XIII (Dante), 42, 50
Eratosthenes, 5
Essai sur la secte des illuminés (Luchet), 13
Essai sur l'indifférence en matière de religion (Lamennias), 98
Essay Towards a Real Character (Wilkins), 81
Ethiopia, 9
Etymologiarum (Isidore of Seville), 28, 44, 59
etymology, 98, 105–6, 107, 111, 115
Euclid, 5
Eudoxius, 5
Eugene IV (pope), 9
Eve, 25, 35–36, 77
evident and multiple borrowing thesis, 111, 113
exchange, cultural, 53
Explication de l'arithmétique binaire (Leibniz), 70

falsehood: Force of the False, 3; leads to truth, viii; verisimilitude and, 17–21
Fama Fraternitatis R.C., 10
Fenius, school of, 29

Ficciones (Borges), 94
Finnegans Wake (Joyce), 95
flat earth theory, 4–7, 18, 21
Fludd, Robert, 11
Foigny, Gabriel de, vii, 93; Austral land, 77; Austral language, viii, 80; imperfect language, ix
Foucault, Michel Paul, 93
Frederick I, 9
Freemasons, 13. *See also* Masons; Templars
Fu-hsi, 74

Gaelic language, 28–29
Galileo, 4
Garibaldi, Giuseppe, 14
Gautier, Jean François, 20
Genette, Gérard, 97
Genot-Bismuth, Jacqueline, 49–50
Geography: Its History and Concepts (Holt-Jensen), 7
Geography (Ptolemy), 65
Gerando, Joseph Marie de, 92
Gilles, Pieter, 80
Giuseppe Balsamo (Dumas), 15
God (Chomskian), 40, 77
God (Hebrew), 2, 23, 24, 28, 35, 39, 40, 51, 55, 70, 77, 79, 108; first spoken words, 36; names of, 42–44, 47–48
gods, belief in, 2
Godwin, Francis, 80
Goedsche, Hermann, 15
grammar, 77–78, 81, 90–91, 102; (*locutio secundaria*), 32, 34;

Modistae, 39, 46; transcendental particles, 87
grammar of ideas, 93
Grand Rabbi, speech of, 15–16
Greek culture, 53–54
Greek language, 26–29, 32, 102, 104, 109
Guichard, Estienne, 79
Gulliver's Travels (Swift), 80

Ham, 25, 66
Heaven of the Fixed Stars, 23
hebdomad, 100
Hebrew language: of Adam, 30, 41–42, 45, 64; Dante and, 32–33; as first language, 39, 46, 49, 101–2; Jesus and, 28, 38; as perfect language, 40, 42, 56; as primordial language, 27, 77, 95; as proto-language, 47; as sacred language, 27–28, 40, 46–47, 49
Heidegger, Martin, 98
heliocentric hypothesis, 4
Heloise, 1
Henry IV (England), 9
hermeneutics, 27
Hermes Trismegistus, 58, 61, 66, 74
Herodotus, 49
Hesiod, 102
Hexaemeron (Basil), 59
Hexaemeron (Saint Ambrose), 59
hexagrams, 70–74
Hieroglyphia sive de sacris Aegypto-rum aliarumque gentium literis (Valeriano), 60
Hieroglyphica (Horapollus), 56–58

Hieroglyphica (Philippos), 58
hieroglyphs, 56–59, 61–62, 102; ideograms as, 66–67
Hillel of Verona, 48–50
Historia animalium (Aristotle), 60
Historia natural y moral de las Indias (Acosta), 67
Historical essay endeavouring the probability that the language of the empire of China is a primitive language (Webb), 64
History of Planetary Systems from Thales to Kepler (Dreyer), 5
History of the Warfare of Science with Theology in Christendom (White), 7
Holt-Jensen, A., 7
Homer, 18, 102
Horapollus, 56–61
Humboldt, Wilhelm von, 77

I Ching, 70–74
iconography. *See* hieroglyphs
ideal societies, 10
Idel, Moshe, 45
ideograms. *See* hieroglyphs
Illuminati of Bavaria, 14
Immanuel of Rome, 49, 50
India, 8, 99–100
Indo-European hypothesis, 97
Inferno (Dante), 33, 41
Institutiones divinae (Lactantius), 5
intelligence versus stupidity, ix
Irish. *See* Gaelic language
Isidore of Seville, 6, 27, 28, 44, 59, 98, 105
Isis, 66

Jacobins, 14, 101
Japeth, 25
Jerusalem, 2, 7
Jesuits, 14–15, 54, 64–65, 68
Jesus Christ, 2, 64
Jewish-masonic plot, 14
"Jews, Masters of the World"
    (Goedsche), 15
John of Holywood, 6
Joly, Maurice, 15, 16
Joyce, James, 95
Juif errant (Sue), 15
Julian the Apostate, 99–100

Kant, Immanuel, 20
Kircher, Athanasius, 61–69, 74, 79,
    102
koine, 26
Krishna, 99

La Terre Australe connue (Foigny),
    80
labyrinth, 93
Lactantius, 5
Lamennais, Hughes-Félicité-
    Robert de, 98
land of novels, 93, 95
Landa, Diego de, 67
language: ability and, 32–33; arti-
    ficial, 103; creation myth, 24;
    dialects, 30; errors, vii; evolu-
    tion of, 102; fictional inven-
    tions in, vii–viii; genius of,
    103–4, 109; historical-cultural
    phenomenon of, 114; Indo-
    European, 97; matrix of, 97;
    natural, 40, 103; nature of,

97–99; order of ideas in, 27;
    philosophic and a priori,
    79–95, 103, 107; plurality of,
    25, 26; rational, 30; sacred,
    26–28, 40, 47, 49, 57–59; uni-
    versal, 26–28, 39–40, 63–64,
    68–69, 78–79, 93. *See also*
    Adamic language; linguistics;
    individual languages
language, perfect, 107–8; Dante
    and, viii, 30, 41–42; Egyptian
    as, 61, 63; Hebrew as, 40, 42,
    56; search for, vii, 55–56, 77, 98
*Language, Torah, and Hermeneutics
    in Abraham Abulafia* (Idel), 45
Latin language, 26–28, 79, 102,
    103–4; grammar, 30, 87
Le Contemporain, 15
Le Goff, Charles, 51
Leibniz, Gottfried Wilhelm, 30,
    53, 69–70, 74, 78, 92
Leopold I (emperor), 68
Les estats et les empires de la lune
    (Bergerac), 80
Les estats et les empires du soleil
    (Bergerac), 80
Les Juifs, nos contemporains
    (Bournand), 5
Les mots et les choses (Foucault), 93
Lettre à Dacier (Champollion), 62
Leucippus, 6
L'harmonie étymologique des langues
    (Guichard), 79
L'Histoire des Sevarambes (Vairasse),
    80
linguistic matrix, 46
linguistics, 88, 107; Dante and, 30,

35, 36; enlightened, 97; lunatic, viii; science of, 97. *See also* language
lions, 62
Locke, John, 78
Lodwick, Francis, 78, 81, 90
Logos, universality of, 26
Luchet, marquis de, 13
Lull, Ramon, 78, 86
Lully, Raymond, 30
L'Univers existe-t-il? (Gautier), 20
Luther, Martin, 24

Machiavelli, Niccolò, 15–16
Macrobius, Ambrosius Theo-dosius, 6
Maier, Michael, 11
Maimonides (Moses ben Maimon), 46
Maistre, Joseph de, vii, 14, 97–115 passim
Man in the Moone (Godwin), 80
Mani (Manichaeus), 14
Marco Polo, 9, 53–54, 56, 63, 65, 74
Martianus Capella, 6
Marvin, F. S., 7
Masons, 13–14, 100; Scottish Rite, 13, 98, 103. *See also* Templars
mathematics, 69–74, 78, 100
matrix languages, 97
Mechanization of the World Picture (Dijksterhuis), 5
Mémoires pour servir à l'histoire du jacobinisme (Barruel), 14
Mendoza, Juan Gonzalez de, 63

mentalese language, 93
Mercury (Wilkins), 63
Merleau-Ponty, Maurice, 50
Mersenne, Marin, 78, 90–91
Messiah, 2, 47
metaphorical expression, 86–87, 89, 100, 102–3
metonymy, 87
Mexican civilizations, 67
mimologism, 97
Minerva, 56
Modistae, 39–40, 46
monogenetic hypothesis, 98, 103
monogeneticists, 98, 105
Montesquieu, 15
Montfaucon, Bernard de, 5
Mophtha, Sacred, 62
More, Thomas, 80
morphemathic functions, 90
morphological rules, 105
Moses, 61
Les Mystères de Paris (Sue), 15
Les Mystères du peuple (Sue), 15
myths, 18–20, 29, 65, 100; creation, 23–24, 29; Eldorado, 19; golden age, 101; Masons, 14; unicorn, 54–55, 75

Name Giver, 24, 111
Napoleon III, 15–16
Naturalis Historia (Pliny), 59
neologisms, 88–89
Nilus, Sergej, 17
Nimrod (Charles James Apperley), 33
Nimrud, 100
Noah, 25, 64, 66

Nomothete (Name Giver), 24
Nouveaux essais sur l'entendement humain (Leibniz), 92
Nova collectio patrum et scriptorum graecorum (Montfaucon), 5
Novissima Sinica (Leibniz), 70
numbers, 56, 78, 92, 100

Obeliscus Pamphilius (Kircher), 62
obscure borrowing thesis, 111, 112
Oedipus Aegyptiacus (Kircher), 61–62, 65–67
Okhrana (political police), 16
Old Man of the Mountain, 14
Oresme, Nicolas, 6
Origen, 6, 59
original iconism thesis, 111, 113
Oscan language, 79
Osiris, 62
Other Inquisitions (Borges), 93

paradise: Dante, viii, 41; languages of, vii. *See also* Eden, Garden of
Paradise (Dante), 23, 30, 41–43, 49, 50
paralogisms, 104
Parmenides, 5
parody, 80–81
particles, transcendental, 87–88
Peirce, Charles Sanders, 19
perfumed panther, 40
periphrases, 86
Perush Havdalah de-Rabbi 'Akiva, 48
Peyrère, Isaac de la, 64
Philip the Fair, 14

Philippos, 58
philosopher's stone myth, 19
Phoenician navigators, 4
phonograms. *See* hieroglyphs
Piazza Navona (Rome), 63
plagiarism, Goedsche and, 15
Plato, 5, 27, 60, 97, 100, 102, 104
Pliny, 59
Plutarch, 60
polygenetic hypothesis, 97–98, 103
polysemia, 94
Popper, Karl, 18
Porphyry, 59
Prague cemetery ritual, 15
Prester John, 7–9, 17, 55
primigenial language, 97–98, 109
primitives, semantic, 81, 86–87, 89, 90–91, 93
Priscian, 32
Protocols of the Elders of Zion, 16–18, 20
Ptolemy, 3–4, 7, 17–18, 62, 65
Purgatory (Dante), 41
Pythagoras, 5, 54

Quaestia quodlibetalis XIII (Aquinas), 1

Rachovskij, Pyotr Ivanovich (Sergej Witte), 16
Readclif, John. *See* Goedsche, Hermann
Readcliff, Sir John. *See* Goedsche, Hermann
Récherches philosophiques (Bonald), 98

Relacion de las cosas de Yucatan
(Diego de Landa), 67
Retcliffe, Sir John. *See* Goedsche,
Hermann
Reynolds, Barbara, 43–44
Ricci, Matteo, 54, 63, 64
Risorgimento, 14
Rosencreutz, Christian, 10
Rosetta stone, 57, 61
The Rosicrucian Enlightenment
(Yates), 11
Rosicrucian manifestos, 10, 17
Rosicrucians, 18, 21
Rosiello, Luigi, vii, 97
Rousseau, Jean Jacques, 67
Russell, Jeffrey Burton, 4, 7

Sacred Mophtha, 62
Saint Martin, Louis-Claude de,
98
Salamanca, sages of, 4, 6–7
Sapir-Whorf hypothesis, 77
Saussure, Ferdinand de, 34–35
Sayers, Dorothy, 43
Scala, Cangrande della, 42
scholastic age, 6
Scottish Rite. *See under* Masons
Search for a Perfect Language
(Eco), vii
secret societies, 10, 14
Selenite language, 80
serendipity, viii, 7, 53, 74
Servius, 32
Shem, 25
Siger of Brabant, 39
Simone, Raffaele, 98
Simonini (Captain), 14

Soirées de Saint-Pétersbourg
(Maistre), 99, 115
Sophocles, 60
Sperber, Julius, 11
Spinoza, Baruch, 78
Stoics, 26, 46
storks, 58–60
Studies in the History and in the
Method of Sciences (Marvin), 7
stutter, 26, 53
Sue, Eugène, 15–16
Swift, Jonathan, 80
synecdoche, 87
syntagm, 86, 88–89
Systema Theologicum ex prae-
Adamitarum hypothesis (de la
Peyrère), 64
Système Général des Sciences et des
Arts (Alembert), 93

Tao, Great Wheel of, 2
Templars, 13–14, 98, 100, 103. *See*
also Masons
Theater of Illusion, 3
Themis aurea (Maier), 11
Theodosius, 57
Theosophism, 98
Thirty Years' War, 10
Thomas Aquinas, 1, 6–7,
20, 39
Timaeus (Plato), 100
"Tlön, Uqbar, Orbis Tertius"
(Borges), 12–13, 94
Torah, 45
Tower of Babel, 8, 25–26,
29–30, 32, 34–35, 43,
45, 55, 97

tradition: cabalistic, viii; preconceived ideas, 54–55
Troy, 18
truth: versus dogmatic thought, 4; versus error, ix; language and, 98, 106, 108, 115; mystical, 56; and myth, 19; scientific, 3; strength of, 1–2
Tübingen, 11
Turgot, Anne Robert Jacques (Baron de l'Aulne), 14

universals, linguistic, 39
universals, semantic, 77–78, 86
universe, existence of, 20–21, 100
Unknowns, Higher, 15
Unknowns, Superior, 13
Utopia (Thomas More), 80
utopian language, 80, 93–94

Vairasse, Denis, 80
Valeriano, Pierio, 60
Valla, Lorenzo, 7

vernacular languages, 30–34, 37, 40, 44
Vico, Giovanni Battista, 103
Vie de Monsieur Descartes (Baillet), 12
virago, 25
Voltaire (François Marie Arouet), 14

Warburton, William, 67
Webb, John, 64
White, Andrew D., 98
Wilkins, John, 63, 78, 81, 87–90, 93–94, 103
William of Rubruck, 9
Witte, Sergej, 16

Xavier, Saint Francis, 64

Yahoo language, 94
Yates, Francis, 11
Yehuda, Romano, 50

Zerakhya of Barcelona, 48–50
Zoroaster, 66

This book was set in 10/13 BEMBO, licensed from Monotype/Adobe, a facsimile of a typeface cut in 1495 by Francesco Griffo (1450–1518) for the Venetian printer Aldus Manutius (1450–1515). The face was named for Pietro Bembo, the author of the small treatise *De Ætna,* in which it first appeared. The companion italic is based on the handwriting of the Venetian scribe Giovanni Tagliente from the 1520s. The present-day version of Bembo was first introduced by the Monotype Corporation in 1929, under Stanley Morison's supervision. Serene and versatile, it is a typeface of classical beauty and high legibility.

This book was designed by Linda Secondari.
Composed at Columbia University Press by Danielle De Lucia.
Printed and bound at Maple Vail.